Stress-Free

Believers

Stress-Free Believers

Turn Worry into Faith, Turmoil into Peace

Harold Metzel

Hickory Creek, TX

Stress-Free Believers

Turn Worry Into Faith, Turmoil Into Peace

Published by:
10-Talent Believers
10 Shore Haven Lane
Hickory Creek, TX 75065

Library of Congress Control Number: 2011909626

ISBN-10: 0982988303
ISBN-13: 978-0-9829883-0-5

Contents

Preface

Stressed out? In the past couple of years, I met Christians who had been exhausted to the point that they could barely think straight. Stress had mounted up until it stripped them of the ability to decide what action to take or what to do next. Like a person in shock, they felt paralyzed—helpless as a child.

How is it possible for people of faith to become so disheartened?

While ministering at a church in southern California, I met with Jacob and Diane. They described to me what they were dealing with. Jacob had lost his job. They'd missed two months of mortgage payments, and the wolf was knocking at their door.

"We have three young kids," Diane said. "Harold, we just don't know what to do. It seems like every door is closing in on us. I'm scared to death that we're going to end up out in the street. Where is God in all of this?"

Have you ever felt like that?

If you're feeling the pressure that's brought your thinking to a standstill, you need not remain imprisoned in that state. You can overcome those feelings and take charge of *whatever* is happening in your life. This book provides the steps to do so.

We've been taught, "*If God is for us who can be against us?*"[1] That not only sounds great, it's true. Yet Jesus explained that "*the cares of this world ... choke the word.*"[2] *The pressures of life can shut down our faith.* Those stressed-out Christians admitted they didn't know what to do.

Let me relate how I encountered those people.

For 25 years, I served in Christian ministry as a pastor, a missionary, and eventually as president of a Bible college. Circumstances in my life then propelled me into a career in the field of finance, tax avoidance, and estate planning. The combination of those two vocations produced a blend of both pastoral and financial perspective.

Upon retiring from employment, I felt the Lord prompting me to share what I'd learned in those financial disciplines. So, for the past eight years, I've conducted seminars in local churches. The two days following every seminar, I'd then meet with each one who requested an individual appointment to discuss his or her financial situation.

In those meetings, I discovered a zone of major concern which spread far beyond the area of just finance. Although some of the people I met wanted to learn more about financial strategies to benefit family or church, many were looking for an escape route—a way out. Often, our conversation led to their admitting bleak situations in other areas of life as well.

As I have nothing to sell, don't manage money, and am not available for hire, meeting with me privately provided them an opportunity to talk with someone safe. Since I also wasn't connected to their community or church, they were assured of confidentiality. And I was invited in behind closed doors where stress had taken over. Many expressed relief after openly disclosing their anxieties.

The motivation to write this book came from observing the enormous stress these fellow believers were going through: threats of losing jobs, homes, even their entire financial base. Developments in this country, extending throughout the whole world, have created a stress-producing engine which has given birth to near panic, even for Christians. When we add to that the "normal" stress we face in all other areas of life, we can feel crushed.

Can you relate to that?

That's not God's plan, on the other hand, for those of you who walk with Him. Not only is it possible for you to live the abundant life that Jesus promised, it's also within reach. As you apply the principles set forth in this book, no matter what problems come your way, you can work your way through them without losing control.

After we had discussed how to handle stress, people were surprised to learn that they *did* know what to do. Most people, I've found, don't need advice. What they needed was to learn (1) how to separate the stress from the problem, and (2) how to ignite once again the faith that can move mountains. *They* learned how. And so can you.

Introduction

Living stress-free is not a fantasy. Of course, stress may be a good or bad thing. When it serves as an indicator, like the warning lights in a car, it's good. When it creates anxiety, like when a fire alarm goes off, it's bad.

Unhealthy stress is neither useful nor God's plan. While no one is exempt from the normal and ongoing pressures of life, when the level of stress rises beyond a certain point it becomes a tyrant. When that happens, you begin to feel you're losing control. "What's going to happen to me?" "What will come of this?" Although stress can be a helper, it can also wreak havoc in your life. As it escalates, it turns more and more into a bully —intimidating you, scaring you, and making you cower. It can get nasty. It can make you sick. Stress can kill.

Loss of employment, marital conflict, credit card debt, and legal troubles are situations that happen to good people. In this book, you'll find ways to relieve most of that unhealthy stress. Your problems won't disappear. But learning how to release that pressure will allow you to walk through those turbulent times with greater composure. You'll increase your ability to travel through life with greater peace and confidence, thus, enabling you to make better decisions.

If we're ever to live as financially prosperous believers, we must shake loose of our paralysis. In the three parts of this book, we'll cover the steps needed to get rid of unhealthy stress:

Part One: Dethroning the Stress-Bully

- By learning how to separate the stress from the problem, we can face difficult situations with the believer's most important tool.

Part Two: God's Role

- Once we understand God's plan and how we can expect Him to participate in our daily activities, we learn when to take our hands off a problem.

Part Three: The Believer's Role

- By accepting the role we were created to fill, God can bring to fulfillment His design for our lives.

Note:

When pressures mount, it's common to feel all alone—isolated. You may feel guilty and even wonder if the trouble you're experiencing represents punishment. Having an opportunity in a group setting to discuss those pressures provides both help and assurance. First, it's healthy to talk things through from various points of view. It's also assuring to see that others struggle with similar issues.

Do you belong to a home group, Sunday School class, or other small group gathering? If so, you might suggest studying this book together. If you're not part of such a group, do you have a close friend or two who might agree to join you in reading a chapter a week and then discussing it over coffee?

The lessons and truths we learn are transformed into tools we can use when we have a chance to discuss how the principles can be applied. Many pastors encourage small group involvement in the belief that we grow stronger and faster when we share our thoughts.

And at the end of each chapter, you'll find the discussion questions stimulating. Additional resources are also available at www.StressFreeBelievers.com. If you allow these helps to start a conversation. you'll find the lessons in this book more beneficial and also more fun.

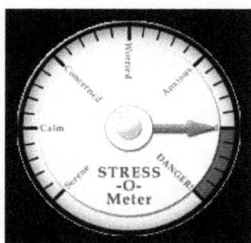

Part One

Dethroning the Stress Bully

Overview

What role does stress play in affecting your emotions, decisions, and ultimately the effectiveness of your life?

When your personal stress meter registers up into the hazardous "red zone," it's warning you of danger: something's out of whack. Performing an effective examination of where the trouble lies requires knowing ourselves thoroughly. Not just our physical side, but the other factors that play into who we've now become.

The first thing we'll examine is our dual nature as believers. The Scripture tells us when God washed away our sins, we came from the Darkness into the Light. We now must learn to live as new creatures. Living in a physical body with a newly born spirit causes us to function as citizens of two very different worlds. Our bodies desire carnal pleasures, while our spirit longs for holiness and intimacy with God. The tendency to revert to prior ways of thinking can hinder our growth.

So we'll take a look into our toolboxes and examine our tools:

- Faith
- Sufficient courage to act on that faith
- The ability to overcome unbelief

The really good news is that the believer's tools already reside in everyone born of God's Spirit. Just like a carpenter or plumber, however, we must come to understand the purpose of each tool and then gain experience in using each one. Ever-expanding pressure sometimes causes our faith and confidence to end up buried so deep that God can seem far away and uncaring. But don't ever accept that as the truth. Remember this verse: *"Cast all your care upon Him, for He cares for you."* (1 Peter 5:7)

Conquering unhealthy stress is not only possible, it's also not difficult. "Oh, really?" Yes, really! It's like changing a bad habit. (Although, admittedly, even that's not *easy!*) Yet it's a whole lot easier than steeling yourself for battle. For like the bogeyman under the bed, the real culprit isn't the situation you face. It's the fear of "What if?"

Taking control of stress, however, does require that you admit to its tyranny. Recognize what it's doing to you. Coming to grips with unhealthy stress requires knowing that it's an enemy.

Here's an important axiom:

> Stress causes worry, worry creates fear, and fear is the opposite of faith.
> When we worry, we're not trusting God. It's a signal that we're afraid; we fear He won't come through for us.

Admitting you're worried or afraid is the starting point. When you say, "I'm worried or afraid about *this*," it identifies the specific battlefield you're entering. You're declaring war against the tormentor which has threatened you on this particular front. God hears that battle cry, and you'll not fight alone. Even as God said to King Jehoshaphat, "*Do not be afraid nor dismayed ... for the battle is not yours, but God's.*" (2 Chronicles 20:15)

Discover More Online

Additional Resources:

- Expanded Articles for Each Chapter
- DVD for Small Group Discussion
- 10 Best Stress-Busting Bible Verses
- 5-CD Audio Book
- Kindle, mp3, and More Downloads
- Signup for "Stress-Free Finances"
  (Soon-to-be-Released Follow-Up Book)

www.StressFreeBelievers.com

Chapter 1

Looking at Life from Both Sides

Then Jesus spoke to them again, saying, "I am the light of the world. He who follows Me shall not walk in darkness, but have the light of life."

(John 8:12)

You're about to learn one of the most amazing benefits of the Christian life. God has given to those who trust Him a tool with the capacity to absolutely dethrone the stress monster. That tool is faith, and it was embedded in you when you became a Christian.

Learning to develop and use our newfound faith takes time as we mature in our Christian walk. And the primary obstacle opposing the growth of faith is our dual nature—carnal and spiritual—that lives within us. Let's consider how your dual citizenship in this world impacts your life every day.

Joni Mitchell wrote the lyrics of this song which Glenn Campbell then made into a hit:

> *"I've looked at life from both sides now,*
> *From win and lose and still somehow,*
> *It's life's illusion I recall.*
> *I really don't know life at all."*[3]

These lines carry new meaning to those of us who've been born again. Life is no longer just a matter of "win and lose." It's the discovery of the eternal side of life that truly matters. That discovery, though, doesn't remove us from the darkened alleys of the world's way of thinking.

We began our lives in a single dimension. We couldn't see into the other side until God's Spirit turned on the Light. We then embarked into a new life in Christ but continue to live in a sinful world. As we now walk the earth with a dual citizenship, it's important to remain aware of the ungodly, magnetic pull to think and behave in the old, most familiar ways.

Note: If you've been a believer for a long time, the principles in this chapter may be quite familiar. Still, take the time to set them in your mind once more. It's from these concepts that we develop the boldness to act on what God says.

New believers, consider memorizing the Bible quotes so you can remind yourself of what God has said and promised. Alternatively, print out from the website

*www.StressFreeBelievers.com, "Harold's 10 Best
Stress-Busting Verses", and review them regularly.*

Stumbling in the Dark

Every living person has asked himself what life is about at some time or another. I remember bringing up the question when I was sixteen, walking along the streets of Chicago with my girlfriend, Donna.

"Do you believe in God?" I asked.

"Sure, don't you?" Donna had been raised Catholic. I hadn't been raised in church at all.

I continued to probe, "Well, why do you suppose He created us then? Are we an alternate version of the ants down there on the sidewalk? Just a side show for God to watch and amuse Himself with?"

Until we call out to God to remove the problem of sin which separates us from Him, we're relegated to stumbling in the Dark and wondering what life's really about. A person who's always been blind cannot imagine light.

And, by the way, it's not a matter of being "too thick" to get it. Nor is the problem one of being too lazy to seek the truth. Consider Buddha, Mohammed, and the Jewish Pharisee Nicodemus, all of whom spent their entire lives seeking spiritual enlightenment. Each of those men discovered one or another means of obtaining at least a *type* of inner peace. That, however, does not turn on the true Light which Jesus talked about. That Light, Jesus explained, comes only one way:

> *"Most assuredly, I say to you, unless one is born again, he cannot see the kingdom of God."*
>
> (John 3:3)

Naturally, that makes sense to those of us who have experienced it. But what did you think about being born again before taking the plunge? We've all listened to friends and even professional comedians make fun of the idea. I have to confess, I did so myself! If it were just comedians poking fun at our beliefs, that would be understandable. They're paid to make us laugh. And friends are going to rib us no matter what we do.

But what about those people we consider leaders, great thinkers, and mentors? What about the people we hire to teach our children or write textbooks? When people in those categories denigrate our faith, it results in more serious consequences. Rabbi Daniel Lapin nails the state of affairs:

> Some universities teach their students that faith in the Bible might be fine for foolish and uneducated folk, but not for those with penetrating minds and advanced degrees. I am always astounded by that type of statement.
>
> What happened to intellectual humility? To dismiss Bible believers like Sir Isaac Newton, scientist Johannes

Keppler, and yes (Rabbi) Don Isaac Abarbanel as less brilliant than oneself, takes quite some hubris. [4]

Outstanding teachers and leaders with brilliant minds may impress us with their intellectual ability, but they still will never understand a Light they've not seen. Will you allow the caustic comments or diatribes of those who remain in the Dark to rattle your faith when they speak from the only perspective they have?

Help your children to take a stand. Remind them often that they, too, hold a dual citizenship in this world. This awareness safeguards us and them against the foolish things the educated, yet unenlightened, may declare as truth.

For although we belong to God and have had the Light turned on, we continue to live in an environment that functions largely in the Dark. Make no mistake. The culture of that Darkness will continue to affect each of us. Bishop Kenneth C. Ulmer addresses this point as he writes:

> The spirit of the world is one of the perennial enemies of the believer. World refers to the world system —to all its values, mind-set, philosophies of life, and priorities that run contrary to the will and way of God. The world suggests that your success requires you to turn away from the path of godliness—to neglect developing your relationship with God. But Jesus said a life without

God or the things of God is worthless, regardless of its appearance. (Mark 8:36)[5]

Walking in the Light

Overcoming the constant pull to revert to the thinking and behavior of our previous, one-dimensional life requires learning to walk in the Light. So often, we spend time going to church, reading the Bible, and learning to trust what God has said, but we hesitate to plunge in and *walk* in His Light. It can seem like moving to a foreign country where not only the language is different but also the habits and even the thinking.

As for me, it took a while to learn to act and talk "Christian." Those of you fortunate enough to have been born into a home with Christian parents are far ahead of the game. It's not that you'll have more Light than any other person. But you have the advantage of *not* having been so completely sold out on the world's thinking that it appears foolish to trust in God. If you were true to your upbringing, you'll also have avoided developing many bad habit patterns others struggle with.

My personal conversion was a dramatic one, like the Apostle Paul's. An "on-the-road-to-Damascus" type of transformation. One day I was living an out-of-control life, trying to experience everything possible. Immediately after calling on God, my life changed so drastically that people were astounded and wondered what had happened to me.

In fact, the year before becoming a Christian, I applied to the General Electric Company to enter an apprentice program and was rejected. The year following my conversion I applied again and was accepted. As I began the program, the director said to me, "I don't know what's happened to you, Harold. Last year, there wasn't a chance. This year, something's different." Of course the difference was that God had been bringing my life to increasing health for almost a year.

Let me tell you another incident. Shortly after going to Japan as a missionary, I enrolled in a language school. While there, I became good friends with Norman who was also a missionary. He once told me he envied the strong and dramatic testimony of how radically God had changed my life. He'd grown up in a Christian home and felt his testimony was insipid.

Many years have now passed. If I could lay our lives out, side-by-side in some graphic way, it would be obvious how much more faithful and centered Norman has been. Who do you think is the more envious now?

Having Dark-side thinking engrained into your thought patterns is a terrific disadvantage. Both of my sisters had become Christians before I did. Whenever they would talk to me about what God had done in their lives, encouraging me to ask Jesus into my life, I remember bracing myself with a determination to not listen. I heard the words but had closed my mind. I've seen others do the same. Why? What are we afraid of?

It is, after all, the *good news* of the Gospel of Jesus Christ.

For me, I know the fear was that I'd miss out on all the fun—the good things life could offer. I wanted freedom without restraint. And so, for several years, not only did I indulge in every pleasure offered me but also pushed the envelope to find more. Of course, there's never *enough* regardless of how much more you find. And oh, what a price I ended up paying.

It's true, my conversion brought about a remarkable change in me, immediately. But there's the quicksand I crawled out of that I'd so willingly hastened to enter: It had set before me a long, difficult route of changing my thought patterns. God has never forsaken me, but I remain ashamed of how many times I embarrassed myself along the way.

It may seem that nothing dramatic happened in your life when you stepped into the Light. Maybe you were even a child when you did so. Yet, if you're diligent in maturing—becoming "perfected" in your faith—you'll outrun the others who started later in their walk with the Lord.

The thinking of the Dark side may still affect you. There's no way out of that for any of us until Jesus comes again and takes us with Him.

Awareness of the tug-of-war pull between the Darkness and the Light will, nonetheless, help you make better decisions. And for those of us who had a more difficult beginning? We may bounce off the walls a bit more, but God is just as faithful to stabilize us in our walk.

Each of us can relate to the words of the poet, Robert Frost:

> *"Two roads diverged in a wood, and I—*
> *I took the one less traveled by,*
> *And that has made all the difference."*[6]

Many around us will not understand the path we travel. How could they?

That path is also not an easy one upon which to stay centered. How could it be?

Yet, Jesus declares it to be the road that leads to eternal life. While we live in this world and must deal with both sides of life, we do so with His promise, *"In the world you will have tribulation; but be of good cheer, I have overcome the world."* (John 16:33)

A New Way of Living

You are no longer the same person you once were. You may not feel much different at first, but the Bible makes it clear in 2 Corinthians 5:17: *If anyone is in Christ, he is a new creation; old things have passed away; behold, all things have become new.*

Can you believe it? *Do* you believe it?

Many of us accept the fact that God has forgiven our sins. We also have at least some confidence that we'll one day go to heaven. But how can that be when we are acutely aware of our "unholiness"? The Bible gives us this hope:

> *Let patience have its perfect work, that you may be perfect*
> *and complete, lacking nothing.*
>
> (James 1:4)

Perfect? Really? It helps to understand that the word "perfect" in that verse may also be translated as "mature." Ah! That makes me feel better. I may never achieve perfection, but I certainly hope to continue maturing.

This new way of living takes practice: resisting the natural inclinations and exercising faith. When we do, God's power in our lives becomes more evident and our faith grows.

The Bible says that every believer still sins, at least sometimes.[7] You may hate the truth of that, yet the struggle between your flesh and your spirit never stops. But don't give up—it's for sure that God won't.

> *For it is God who works in you*
> *both to will and to do for His good pleasure.*
>
> (Philippians 2:13)

Concluding Thought ...

Isn't that exciting? It is *God* who works in you. Not only to accomplish (or do) His will, but He also provides the "want to" (or will). Think of that! You don't have to pump yourself up. Even your desire to please Him and overcome sin relates to God's Spirit working within you.

Resting in the confidence that God now lives within you and will provide the power you need to to fulfill His purpose in your life is the first ingredient to dethroning the stress bully. Once your spirit has been quickened and made alive by the Holy Spirit, an entirely new dimension becomes available, whether you feel it or not.

Life from Both Sides

For Discussion:

- Share what the Dark side of life was like for you.

- Tell about your conversion. Did it dramatically change you, or has your growth been more gradual?

- Have you, like Norman, envied someone else's experience? If so, who was that, and why the envy?

- Discuss your confidence, or lack thereof, that God will complete the work He started in you.

- Talk about your experience with a "dual citizenship." Both the blessings and the pitfalls.

What Action Steps Can You Take?

-
-
-
-

Chapter 2

How Significant Is Your Faith?

"Faith is believing in things when common sense tells you not to."[8]

-- George Seaton

Faith is a tool. Every tool you'll ever see was created for a specific purpose. The person who uses a screwdriver as a chisel—or a knife as a can opener—either doesn't have the proper tool or may not know the right tool to use. Using these unsuitable tools often results in two outcomes: a butchered-up job and a damaged screwdriver or knife. When the correct tool is used for each job, every task becomes easier and more efficient.

The word "apprentice" refers to a person learning to use the tools of a given profession. When the apprenticeship is completed, he or she will handle each tool with confidence and skill. Have you ever watched an artisan at work? They make the job look so easy, and the final product is beautiful. That artisan acquired both the demonstrated knowledge and skill in one way —practice.

The Substance of Your Faith

If our faith is ever to become effective and comfortable in our hands, we must come to understand it; that is, know when to use it and how to apply it. We've got to lay that tool out on our bench and study it. So, let's do that.

Another word for faith is trust. It may help to move away from the spiritual application of faith for a moment. Who do you trust the most? "Well," you might say, "I trust a number of people." Picking out one person isn't a satisfying answer. You trust one person most in *this* situation, but a different person in *that* one. Why is that?

Trust is based on the character, knowledge, and skill of an individual. As each person has a different blend of those attributes, we place our faith in different people depending on what we're trusting them for.

My daughter is a nurse. When completing a legal document giving power of attorney for someone to make healthcare decisions for me, in the event I become incapable of doing so myself, I choose her. In addition to her training as a nurse, she can be very practical when it comes to life and death decisions. She loves me as much as anyone, but I trust that she also has the ability to set aside her emotions if it comes to deciding whether or not to "pull the plug." Not everyone can make that kind of decision without feeling guilty. In other areas, I implicitly trust my wife, or my son, or my best friend, and so on. Trusting, or having faith, means we have confidence that someone will (or will not) behave in a certain way.

Now, let's move the study of this "trust" tool back onto the spiritual application. When we talk about having faith, we normally mean having faith in God. What can you and I trust God to do? And, on the flip side, what are we confident He will not do?

For sure, it's a giant leap to move from trusting people to trusting God. We are, after all, talking about *God*: the Great I Am, the One who does not change, the One who cannot lie. When He speaks, it's done: a universe is created, galaxies appear, life springs into existence. Of *course* we can trust Him to do whatever He says He will do or will not do.

Yes, but based on what? His character. We trust people because of their reliability, we trust God the same way. And in His case, He doesn't change or vary. So, the better you know God, the more you'll trust Him. The more experience you have with Him, the more you'll have faith in Him. How do we get to know Him better? In the same way we get to know people, we've got to spend time with Him. Whether that time is spent in church, in prayer, Bible reading, sharing with other believers, or in any other way—our faith grows as our experience with Him deepens.

Now let's move to the practical side. How do we *use* this faith, this tool? From the Scripture we know that without faith it's impossible to please God.[9] We also know Jesus said that whatever we ask in prayer, believing, we would receive.[10]

The only exception to that is found in James 4:3: *"You ask and do not receive, because you ask amiss."* So let's put this into a single concept. If we ask God for anything we know is *not* against His will or character (James calls this "asking amiss"), we will have what we ask for, if we believe. Is there any other way to interpret the verse? What's more, when we do that, God is pleased.

Allow me to add a couple of reminders to qualify that interpretation. (And no, I'm not backpedaling.)

First, Jesus said we would have what we asked for. He did not say that we'd experience a miracle. I'm sure you've undoubtedly discovered many things in your life that have indeed come to pass. You prayed for them at an earlier time, but they didn't jump into existence right at the same moment. And yet when we pray with faith, spiritual power is released. Whether we pray for unbelieving loved ones, for healing, or against spiritual wickedness,[11] something happens right away. The end result we long to see may not yet be in existence, but it's already on its way.

Miracles do happen *sometimes*, like when Peter walked on the water. Was he demanding a miracle? I don't think so. Neither was Jesus trying to prove a point or teach a lesson. If we take the story at face value, Peter was simply astonished that there was the Lord, outside of their boat on the water. Not sure if his eyes were playing tricks on him, he simply said, *"Lord, if it is You, command me to come to You on the water."*[12] Jesus answered simply, *"Come."* And Peter walked on the water. Voila! A miracle. It wasn't contrived, it wasn't expected, it just happened within God's timing.

The next reminder is that we ask according to God's will; that is, in harmony with His character. Jesus said we are to pray that God's will be done on earth as it is in heaven.[13] Just as we learn to trust God to a greater extent once we're assured of His reliability, we come to genuinely *know* Him with increasing intimacy in the same way. By getting to know Him, not only through His Word but also through our life's experiences, we become confident that what we ask is in agreement with His will.

When we pray with that kind of confidence, the Faith Tool brings new things into existence:

> *Faith is the confidence that what we hope for*
> *will actually happen;*
> *it gives us assurance about things we cannot see.*
>
> (Hebrews 11:1, NLT)

The significance of faith is that it releases spiritual power, God's power, into our world. Whether or not we choose to be people of faith is up to us. When we choose in favor of exercising faith, God is pleased. When we choose to live without expecting God to invade our lives, He gives us that freedom, but we remain spiritually immature.

The Faith You Now Have is Enough

For nearly all my life I felt as if my faith were in short supply, certainly not *enough*, especially at those times when I was sick, or didn't have enough money, or a job. In other words, when my stress level was high, right then is when I most needed faith, but I didn't feel spiritual or full of faith at all. In fact the opposite was true. I felt depleted, empty.

Of course, most of us *call* on God when we're sick, needy, or in trouble. But having full faith and confidence that He will answer seems elusive when the pressure is on.

How much faith do you have right now? How much do you need to have? Before we move on with ways to ignite our faith, it's important to see clearly that the faith you now have is enough.

Enough for what? For whatever you need.

Prior to my conversion, I honestly didn't think I had what it takes to become a Christian. My sisters and the girl I was dating shared their testimonies and encouraged me to give it a try. But I just didn't believe. It sounded like silly mysticism to me.

Nonetheless, one day my girlfriend invited me to attend a special church service at which a man from Youth for Christ was going to speak. At the conclusion of his message, he invited those who had not yet asked Christ in their heart to come to the altar, and I did.

My prayer, on the other hand, was about as strong of a statement of *unbelief* as you can imagine. I prayed, "God, if there is a God, I don't think I can be a Christian. But that preacher just said that sin was the cause of the emptiness in me: that sin is standing in the way of my discovering the true purpose of life. So I ask you to forgive my sins and let Jesus come in."

That was it! Even after the service when my older sister, Lois, was so excited I had come forward, I told her, "I don't think I can do this." Her advice was for me not to worry. I'd done what God said to do. Now it was time for me to just wait and see. My part, she suggested, was to read the Bible and pray every day and go to church as often as I could. In other words, try to draw close to God and learn about Him. Well, I thought, even though I had little faith, those were things I could actually do. So I did them. And what God did in me was a miracle. My life turned around so radically and quickly that both of my unbelieving parents not only stopped all critical remarks about Lois's "religion," they also became Christians.

Get the point? Your story will be a bit different than mine, but at some point you invited God into your life —and He responded. Do you think you have no faith? Or maybe faith that is so small it couldn't be of any value? Your faith couldn't be smaller than mine when I prayed: "God, if there is a God, I don't think I can do this." Even if I didn't think I had enough faith to believe there *was* a God, He answered that faithless call.

Undoubtedly, there are numerous times you've called on God and He answered. If you're like me, you find it frustrating at times when you think like the man who said to Jesus, *"Lord, I believe; help my unbelief!"* [14]

Lord, Help Our Unbelief!

When we step out to trust in what appears not yet to be, just by making a bullheaded decision to trust what God says is true, our faith grows. Will it ever grow to the point that doubt is no longer an issue? Oh, no.

It seems strange, but that's also part of God's plan. As true as it was for Adam and Eve, trusting and obeying what God says is the hallmark of sons and daughters who are capable of representing Him and managing whatever He assigns to them.

Without faith it is impossible to please Him,
for he who comes to God must believe that He is,
and that He is a rewarder of those who diligently seek Him.
(Hebrews 11:6)

Doubt will continue to plague us. It also pesters your pastor and every other spiritual leader. The struggle against trusting our senses instead of God's promises is a life-long struggle for all of us. It's the Dark, fighting the Light.

Just imagine, God *designed* it that way. It isn't enough to simply believe in Him. He wants us to decide over and over again to trust Him rather than our senses. So what can we do about that persistent unbelief which works at wearing us down? It's impossible to keep doubtful thoughts from entering our minds, but there is one remedy which really works: *Don't speak those thoughts of doubt.*

Develop the habit of saying whatever God says is true. Our culture, education, and even our own logic are flawed to some degree. When we state beliefs that are contrary to what God has said, it kills faith.

It may sound harmless to say, "After all, common sense tells you ...," or "I know I should trust God for this but ...." Those statements diminish our faith. They're not harmless. It amounts to speaking and confessing unbelief.

This is why memorizing Scripture is so important; not so you can impress people but so you can easily remember what God has said. Whenever you are tempted to speak from a standpoint of fear, stress, or doubt, just say what God has said is true.

Think of the power released when we combine faith and confession. The Scripture says this:

> *If you confess with your mouth the Lord Jesus and believe*
> *in your heart that God has raised Him from the dead,*
> *you will be saved.*

(Romans 10:9)

If you confess with your mouth and couple that with faith—things happen. It releases spiritual power. Could it be that by fearing what *could* happen, and speaking out of your fear, that you also influence the outcome?

If you can't speak words of faith, just "put your hand over your mouth."[15] When God speaks, things come into or go out of existence. He cannot lie. Therefore, focus on what God says is true in spite of what may appear to be true.

Concluding Thought ...

The tools available to dethrone the stress bully are faith and the courage to act on it. Is your faith enough? Absolutely! Jesus said even if it's as small as a mustard seed, it will move mountains. The faith you now have is more than enough.

In the next chapter, we'll learn how to trigger it into action with courage.

□ □ □ □ □ ⎯

The Significance of Faith

For Discussion:

- Have you ever considered Faith as a tool?
- In what ways will thinking about Faith as a tool help you to apply it?
- Who are the people you most trust? In which areas do you most trust them? How did that trust come about?
- Have you ever seen or experienced a miracle? Can you share the story?
- After reading the chapter, can you see how the faith you now have is enough?
- In what ways have the things you've said undermined faith? How can you apply the idea of "putting your hand over your mouth?"

What Action Steps Can You Take?

-
-
-
-

Chapter 3

Belly Up to the Bully

"Be strong and of good courage; do not be afraid,
nor be dismayed, for the LORD your God
is with you wherever you go."

(Joshua 1:9)

How can we get our faith to apply in the problems of everyday life? How do we ignite it?

God has promised He'll give us all we need, go with us through any situation, and fight for us when our strength is not sufficient. So how do we tap into that? We know what God has promised, but what part are we to play? In many cases, when filled with worry or fear, the only thought in our mind is ... RUN!

Running, of course, is the natural fight-or-flight instinct trying to protect us. The warning light comes on. There's potential danger here. We're smart enough, of course, to realize that running will not solve the problem. So how do we prepare ourselves to fight, especially when there appears to be no real enemy to go after?

Believing in God and putting faith to work are two separate issues. In order for faith to do any good, we must take action based on our belief that what the Bible says is true.

You say you have faith, for you believe that there is one God. Good for you! Even the demons believe this, and they tremble in terror. How foolish! Can't you see that faith without good deeds [the exercise of courage] *is useless? Don't you remember that our ancestor Abraham was shown to be right with God by his actions when he offered his son Isaac on the altar? You see, his faith and his actions worked together. His actions made his faith complete. And so it happened just as the Scriptures say: "Abraham believed God, and God counted him as righteous because of his faith."*

(James 2: 19-23, NLT)

Separate Stress from the Issue at Hand

Let's take a closer look at the story in the above verses.

God promised 100-year-old Abraham a son[16] and then tells him to go make a sacrifice of him, his only son. Well, talk about stress! Now marry that to bewilderment. "What? This can't be for real! God *abhors* human sacrifice."

You and I have the benefit of knowing "the rest of the story." But Abraham didn't! We know that God provided a way out, but He first required Abraham to trust Him and to take action based on that trust.

How can you relate with Abraham's plight? Can you identify with what Abraham must have gone through? "I just don't believe this. What I *thought* I heard certainly couldn't have been God. He wouldn't do that to me." Have you ever mulled over such a thing? I know I have.

Eventually, Abraham realizes that the facts are just what they appear to be. His back is against the wall. He can't run. It would be pointless to argue or fight with God. He simply must come up with a plan of action.

"OK," he tells himself. "Settle down. I've got to quiet my heart or I'll never be able to think." And then he gets his mind into gear. "I know who God is. I know His promises, His character, that He has always provided and cared for me. Often, even when I didn't understand what was going on, He had a purpose which He was leading me toward. So what can I do? What alternatives are available to me?"

Having thought it through, Abraham decides there aren't any "alternatives." He must face the situation and walk through it. It was either that or disobey God.

Let's cut to the end. He bundles up the fire and wood and heads off with Isaac to the sacrifice site on the mountain. Right there, God provides a substitute—

a ram caught in a thicket. Isaac is spared and Abraham has proven he trusts God completely. He's also learned a new lesson and calls the place Jehovah Jireh: "The Lord will provide."

As a review of that story, what steps did Abraham take? Wasn't it—none at first? He was simply dumbfounded, stunned at what loomed before him. Can you relate to that? Next, he realized he had to quiet his pounding heart. He faced a real danger: his long-awaited, precious son's life was at risk. This was no simple warning light. The lights and sirens screamed in his mind. The stress meter quivered, pegged at the top. His mind remained locked on the impending disaster.

He then took time to consider the options. What else could he do? What ways were available to avoid or circumvent the danger facing him? After considering every possibility, he resolved there was only one course of action: obey or disobey. Bracing himself for what he must go through, he prepared what was needed and set out to walk through the fire of the experience.

Let's break it down further still:

1. He faced a threatening tragedy.
2. He realized fear blocked his ability to think.
3. He separated the fear (stress) from the trial at hand.
4. He considered his options, made a decision, and prepared to endure what could not be avoided.

Pause for a moment and reflect on those steps.

Fear often towers above the reality of what's really going on. Anticipating an unpleasant experience can make us sick, immobilize us, or precipitate premature decisions. So, the first step to take when confronted with a problem is to separate the fear from the problem itself.

Worry causes fear, and fear is the direct opposite of faith. That's why Jesus repeatedly taught His disciples—and therefore us—*do not worry*. Your heavenly Father knows what you have need of and will never forsake you. Problems will come. Jesus forewarned us of the reality:

> "[God] *makes His sun rise on the evil and on the good, and sends rain on the just and on the unjust.*"
>
> (Matthew 5:45)

It was never God's intent to shield us from all adversity. It's by learning how to handle those stressful circumstances that develops us into more capable managers. As we learn to face one thing after another, we become less intimidated and more efficient when trouble comes our way. And that, in turn, makes us more valuable to God in His plan for us.

In order to make good decisions with a clear mind, we must depose that stress monster. It's interesting to note how often we cause ourselves stress which isn't even warranted. Earl Nightingale made this observation:

No one is without problems; problems are part of living. But let me show you how much time we waste in worrying about the wrong problems. Here's a reliable estimate of the things people worry about: things that never happened, 40 percent; things over and past that can't be changed by all the worry in the world, 30 percent; needless worries about our health, 12 percent; petty miscellaneous worries, 10 percent; real, legitimate worries, 8 percent.

In short, 92 percent of the average person's worries take up valuable time, cause painful stress—even mental anguish—and are absolutely unnecessary.[17]

When you consider the facts, unrelated to and divorced from the stress, they represent no more than problems to solve or situations you must go through. That may turn out to be unpleasant indeed, but there's life on the other side. We might as well use the tool that is available only to us believers: faith. It is the choice, as George Seaton pointed out, of *"believing ... when common sense tells you not to."*[18]

Confront such a problem first by saying what God says is true instead of visualizing the disaster it portends. And, just like the wicked witch in *"The Wizard of Oz"* when the water was thrown on her, you'll be amazed to find the stress element diminish and melt into a non-threatening puddle.

No matter how big your faith is, the issue will remain. The problem doesn't disappear. But it's now a process to walk through, a challenge to be faced, an obstacle to overcome. No more, no less. Not only can you do it, you will, and you'll face life with a newfound strength. Jesus encouraged:

> *"These things I have spoken to you,*
> *that in Me you may have peace.*
> *In the world you will have tribulation;*
> *but be of good cheer,*
> *I have overcome the world."*

(John 16:33)

Here's the bottom line: Isolating stress from the problem allows faith to disempower it. The indicator light will still blink, but the flashing lights and siren go away.

Exercise Courage

Triggering faith into action, requires that it be linked with courage. Do you have enough courage? That question begs another: "Courage for what?"

Just as we all have *some* faith, we all have *some* courage. Each of us take risks. Sometimes we take big risks, albeit in selected areas. In other areas, we may be extremely reluctant.

In most cases, courage isn't called for in conditions in which we are experienced. People who jump out of airplanes, drive race cars, or climb mountains, do so with confidence once they've gained experience in those exploits.

It's the same in the spiritual realm. You become afraid to trust God when you're facing something you haven't faced before. That's when stress and fear rush in, and God can seem far away. But that doesn't mean either your faith or your courage is gone or inadequate.

The faith *and* the courage you now have are enough, even if they seem so small you often doubt their existence. They both exist, I promise you. Not only are they present, but they're also enough to propel you on a twofold journey of discovering who you really are and exercising the faith you could never have imagined.

Don't think so? Neither did Peter, although he walked on water, healed the sick, and walked out of a jail cell. You may not do those things, but ... then again, who knows? No matter how big the problem, the faith and courage required are small.

Consider how a little faith can blossom into significant faith. The eleventh chapter of Hebrews gives a whole list of examples of people who "by faith" accomplished great things. Some of their acts, however, started with normal everyday-faith. No spiritual giant in sight.

Rahab, for instance, saved her entire household just by agreeing to hide the spies in her house. Abel did nothing more than bring the appropriate sacrifice to God and thereby was commended as a righteous man. It was out of simple acts of obedience and trust like this that men and women such as Noah, Abraham, and Sarah developed their faith. Then one day, they saw God do incredible miracles in their lives. It was by *simple* faith that they saw God's power released in their behalf. And, I believe, so will you.

There are some who try to call down miracles from heaven. (I've tried it myself! But I didn't have much luck.) My personal experience has led me to believe that although it's important to pray prayers of faith, the miracles come at God's timing, not mine. Although I can't call down miracles at will, I've seen several. The first was within months after I became a Christian.

The church in which I came to know the Lord was very small, probably less than 50 people. Every few months, we would gather with churches from other communities to hold a joint service. They called these "rallies." It provided a great way for small churches to gather into a larger group to worship and do fun things. These gatherings were always held on Saturdays.

A number of us young people, who had recently committed ourselves to the Lord, looked forward to these rallies. One time, as we gathered at the church for a car-pool to the hosting city, we received a phone call from Jim, a recent convert and a key member of our group. He was sick, extremely sick, and in no condition to join us.

My older brother-in-law, Everett, said to me, "Why don't we go pray for him? We have time before we pull out." So we jumped in a car and drove about 25 miles to his home. His mother, not a Christian at the time, opened the door. We explained we came to pray for Jim. A bit mystified, she let us in and took us to his room.

There was Jim in bed, flushed with fever and looking pretty bad. When we explained our mission, he told us how much he appreciated our effort and invited us to pray. Everett took out a little vial of oil, anointed Jim, and we prayed.[19] When we finished praying, there was no evidence that anything had happened. Jim looked just as pitiful as when we'd arrived. Nonetheless, he thanked us again for coming.

Everett stood silent for a moment and then said, "Well, get up."

"What?" Jim asked.

"Get up. We didn't just come to pray for you, we came to get you for the rally."

Dumbfounded for about two seconds, it then dawned on him that Everett really meant it. "Oh, OK," he said. "Wait just a minute." He got out of bed, cleaned up, dressed, and in just a little while we were on our way back to our church.

Jim's mother must have thought we were crazy. He didn't look one speck better. He had to hang onto the door jam as he got out of bed and prepared to put his clothes on. He remained just as flushed as when we'd arrived. Getting out of bed caused him to break into a sweat. Never mind, he was going to the rally. What were we doing to her son? And what crazy kind of religious belief had he gotten into?

Here comes the miracle. It took about 40 minutes to drive from Jim's house to our church. By the time we got there, Jim was completely healed. The fever was gone, his color was normal, and he told everyone he didn't feel sick at all. In fact, he was feeling great. Believe me, so were we!

Those sorts of experiences haven't happened very often in my life, but I'm so grateful for those that did. They've helped me learn so much about faith, miracles, the lack of miracles, and learning to trust God when evidence is not yet visible.

Concluding Thought ...

Look back at your Christian beginning. The courage each of us exercised when we first came to the Lord was demonstrated by making the decision that "Today, I'm asking Christ into my heart. Today, I'm beginning my life as a believer."

How did you do that? For me, I got out of my seat to kneel at the altar. Some of you will have raised your hand, made eye contact with the pastor, or simply cried out to God in the privacy of a moment to say, "God, today, right now, I'm making a decision." And a new life began for you.

The coupling of faith and the courage to take action work the same in any situation. We first must call on Him, and then obey whatever He has told us to do. That obedience requires the courage to make a decision, act without any guarantee, and rely on His faithfulness.

Do so with confidence. He is, after all, known as "The Faithful and True."

Belly Up to the Bully

For Discussion:

- In what areas of your life have you enjoyed seeing faith work?
- In what areas have you struggled in getting faith to work?
- Can you share an area where stress needs to be removed from a problem in order for you to use the Faith Tool?
- Earl Nightingale suggested that only 8% of our fears are justified. Can you identify one or two you need to let go?
- Talk about courage. In what areas do others consider you courageous? In what areas do you find yourself timid?

What Action Steps Can You Take?

-
-
-
-

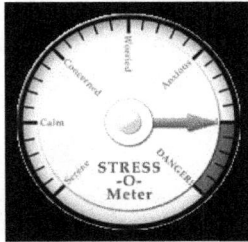

Part I - Dethroning the Stress-Bully

Let's Summarize:

The faith and courage you now have are enough.

1. Enough for what?

    For everything God designed you to become and for every situation you may encounter.

2. Separate the stress from the problem itself.

    That done, focus on the difficulty at hand.

3. Look calmly at the situation.

    Be sure you do not deny the reality of what is.

4. Consider every step which could be taken.

    Then choose how you will manage the issue.

5. Finally, act on that choice.

Remember this adage:

> What is, is. What is not, is not. And no amount of wishing or wanting will change either of those two facts.

The above statement isn't fatalistic but one of adult wisdom. We gain no ground by denying the truth of whatever stands in front of us. God wants us to manage every area of our lives with no more stress than that which is healthy. We must not allow ourselves to be driven by the terror which can come when we fear what may lie ahead.

No matter what problem or difficulty may arise, God has promised to see you through. Lost your job or your home? Going to jail? Diagnosed with an incurable disease? Situations like these can be terrifying. Remember, God has not promised to rescue us from those things. He has, however, promised to see us through if we will trust Him, make good decisions, and act on them.

"What is, is." Set the stress of it aside. Ask God to give you the courage and wisdom to walk through each situation, and you'll come out on the other side stronger and more capable than ever. Make the necessary bullheaded-decision and allow your faith and courage to germinate your seed of faith.

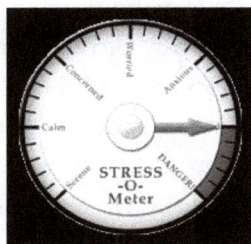

Part Two

God's Role

Overview

How can we cooperate with God in fulfilling His will on earth? When He created the world and all its inhabitants, He had a specific objective in mind. The Bible explains that not only did God make man in His own image, but He also has a plan—a destiny—for His people to achieve. Having created Adam and Eve, God didn't just walk away from the world after creating it. One only needs to read the Bible to see how active God has remained in His relationship with man throughout history.

For God's plan to be completed, we who belong to Him must fulfill our role—but God has a role as well. In His Word, we'll see that there are certain things He said we are to trust Him to do, and other activities that are up to us. Knowing the difference provides wonderful peace.

Unhealthy stress finds an opening in our lives when we aren't sure of what God wants us to do, or of what we can rely on from Him. Before tackling our side of the issue, it's important that we understand God's comprehensive plan.

Note:

Many people, maybe even you, have listened to sermons and teachings about this or that portion of Scripture without first having a sense of what the Bible is about in its entirety. Those snippets impart slices of truth but can leave us with notions that don't sketch out the bigger picture. Allow me to usher you, through the coming chapters, into seeing God's overall plan for you and me.

□ □ □ □ □ _

Chapter 4

Discover God's Comprehensive Plan

*For by Him all things were created that are in heaven
and that are on earth, visible and invisible,
whether thrones or dominions or principalities or powers.
All things were created through Him and for Him.*

(Colossians 1:16)

Most of us have heard some version of "The Blind Men and the Elephant." The original story apparently came from a parable in China around the time of Christ. John Godfrey Saxe turned it into a famous poem by 1873.[20]

Here's a quick review: Six blind men examined an elephant, each feeling a different body part. Each man arrived at a different conclusion: the body felt like a wall, the legs like a tree trunk, the tail like a rope, the trunk like a snake, the tusks like a sword, and the ears like a fan. They all then sat and argued about what the elephant was like, each assured the others were wrong.

The moral of the story is that if we can't see something as a whole, examining only one or more of its parts can lead to mistaken conclusions. This is also true about studying the Scripture or God's character. Many arguments and much confusion arise because people haven't learned to see the entire picture. "Why would a loving God send people to hell?" "Why do the righteous suffer?" "How can God be merciful and good, yet at other times command cruel and destructive action?"

The truth is—God will always be true to His character. He cannot be otherwise. When we're confused, it's because we either do not yet know Him well enough, or we don't understand His overall plan. God created the world and all that's in it for a purpose. When we get the Big Picture, the paradox goes away.

The opening verses of the Bible declare, "In the beginning, God ...."[21] Let's go back to that time. What was in God's mind and heart from the beginning?

If you could have reviewed His schematic or draft for the world, including all of mankind—just before He created anything—what do you think God's plan would have looked like from His point of view?

God is eternal, having neither beginning nor end. Any attempt to grasp His plan must be approached from that perspective. As our lifespan represents just a moment in eternity, attempting to understand God's objectives from the standpoint of just that moment will disclose little. So we need to consider the Bible as a whole.

Here's the concept:

- God made man in His own likeness, entrusting him with the freedom of choice; that is, the ability to make logical and moral decisions.

- Man was created to live eternally. Look carefully and you'll see He's invited us to manage the assets of His kingdom(s), not just in this life but forever.

- Exactly *what* we will manage in our tomorrows depends on how well we've learned to manage what's already been put into our hands. Matthew 25:21 says, *"Well done, good and faithful servant; you were faithful over a few things, I will make you ruler over many things."*

That's *why* we were created. Certainly to worship and live in fellowship with God but also to manage whatever He puts into our hands. Managers are overseers, decision makers. God wasn't just creating another creature. He wants people to worship Him, talk with Him, share and work alongside Him for all of eternity. Yet, even before beginning this enormous endeavor, God anticipated a problem. As a foundation to what we're about to study, let's review that problem to see it from God's viewpoint.

Given a free will, the temptation for mankind to step outside the boundaries would always be present. It was true for Adam and Eve, and it's true for us. With even the best of intentions, every man and woman is tempted to step over the line. "I wonder what *that* would be like?" "That sure looks good." "It wouldn't do any real harm if I ...."

But God is holy. Nothing unclean, deceitful, bent, or dishonest can stand in His presence. That's why the soul that sins will die.[22] It's not because God is rigid or enjoys punishing disobedience. His nature simply disallows it. Nothing impure can exist anywhere near Him. Therefore, in order for His plan to work, God had to design a way of escape, a plan of redemption, some way to salvage lost lives. Having stepped over the line, man could not get back to God on his own. So "before the foundation of the world,"[23] God provided an escape: He determined to pay the price for sin Himself.

Move forward to the present day. The only requirement for us to obtain that remedy now is to want it badly enough to make a decision. The price has been paid. Calling on God to forgive, wash away our sin, and make us clean puts us back inside the line which was crossed. It's the only action needed to bring about redemption. When a person receives Jesus as Savior, he now not only has eternal life promised to him but also has been invited to share authority with God. Second Timothy 2:12, (NIV) says, *"If we endure, we will also reign with Him."* And Revelation 5:9-10 substantiates the prophecy:

"For You (Jesus) were slain, and have redeemed us to God
by Your blood. Out of every tribe and tongue and people
and nation, And have made us kings and priests to our God;
And we shall reign on the earth."

We shall *reign* with him—forever!

Really? That's a phenomenal thought. Mind-boggling!

What do you suppose we'll rule over? That, the Bible teaches, depends on us. Those who are faithful in managing even a little, He will make masters over much. And it is, of course, the theme of this book. But how can we become better managers of all that's under our care, making better decisions, while avoiding the errors caused by the pressures from the stress bully? The first step is to remember Who owns it all.

Settling the Matter of Ownership

We were created to manage not only assets, but relationships, our service to others, and eventually kingdoms. Whoa! Wait a minute! Kingdoms? Have we taken a giant leap in logic?

Nope. Read the above verse from Revelation 5 once again: it says, "kings and priests." I have no more insight into exactly how that will play out than anyone else. That is, however, what the Scripture says. God has really big plans for you and me, albeit within limits. You and I were designed to be both kings and priests, BUT we will never be owners.

> *The earth is the Lord's and everything in it;*
> *the world and all who live in it.*
>
> (Psalm 24:1, NIV)

It can't be stated any clearer: God owns it all. Whatever He allows to come into our hands is only for us to manage—not for us to possess. The same is true for kings and priests. And here we learn the concept of stewardship, or management, in contrast to that of ownership.

Note:

The word steward is an old English word for manager. That's the way it was first translated into English, and it stuck.

So remember, stewardship doesn't pertain to giving. Referring to a fundraising effort as a "stewardship campaign" may sound a little less direct, or maybe a bit more spiritual, but keep the meaning clear in your own mind. In the Bible, steward means manager.

As believers, we acknowledge that we do not now—and will not ever—own anything. When we truly give up ownership, deliberately and intentionally let it go, we become free. Not only free from the drive to possess, but we also discover it changes the way we think. Our mindset is altered to one of faith, trusting *God* to provide, as we manage what He gives us.

A Clear Delineation

Two stories in the Scripture illustrate this contrast.

1) Joseph the Manager

Joseph exemplified the thinking and behavior of a good manager. Having been sold as a slave to wealthy Potiphar, he conscientiously carried out whatever duties he was given. Once Potiphar learned he could rely on him, he gave him increasing responsibility. Eventually, Joseph was in charge of everything in Potiphar's house.

Later, defrauded by Potiphar's wife, Joseph was thrown into prison. Again, he carefully carried out whatever was asked of him. Before long, he was given oversight of everything in the prison.

Finally, when brought before the king to interpret his dream, God gave him the interpretation, and he became second in power in all of Egypt. In each case, starting with only simple tasks to perform, he rose to being authorized to manage everything the real owner possessed.

The story of Joseph illustrates a principle which works in our everyday life as it does in God's kingdom: *If we are faithful and diligent over the small things currently in our hands, more will be given.*

Any employer will attest to this. When a worker distinguishes himself by exceeding the duties of his job, his employer will give added responsibility, authority, and benefits to that worker.

2) The Rich Young Ruler

Standing in contrast, and illustrating the opposite, is the parable of the rich young ruler. Here is a young man who "owned" a lot of things. The story makes it clear he had significant wealth but was also devout in his faith. He kept all the Commandments and had disciplined himself to live as a good man.

Jesus commended him and then answered his question of what else he could do to inherit eternal life. "*Sell all that you have and distribute to the poor ....*"[24] This was more than the young man was willing to do, and he went away sad. It's obvious that this man was skilled at managing significant assets. He'd not only acquired but was also maintaining wealth (often the more difficult part). His problem was this: *he regarded those things as belonging to him.* He was the owner. They were *his* possessions.

Jesus made this clear: it's impossible to serve both God and mammon (money/possessions).[25] Each of us must decide who owns what we hold in our hands. If we view those things as belonging to us, the decisions we make will not be consistent with that of a good steward.

So here we stand with a decision to make: *Are we or aren't we willing to relinquish ownership?* If we will ever become all that God created us to be, the answer to that question must be a clear "Yes." (Can you say "yes" out loud, right now?)

Take an Inventory

What's within your purview, your areas of influence to manage? When you consider not only all of your material assets but all of your relationships and responsibilities, how extensive of an inventory do you come up with? I'll bet it turns out to be quite a lot. Consider this list:

1) Yourself

When it comes to managing almost anything, it boils down to managing ourselves. We must manage how we spend our time, effort, and resources. Will we give a lot of time to this and less time to that; make a commitment to this activity and say no to that? Managing our time, our vocation, personal development, and service to others embodies a lot of decision making.

2) Relationships

Neglected relationships stagnate. When we stop communicating with people, even those we love dearly, the closeness subsides. People we were close to years ago will still take our calls and be glad to hear from us, but the intimacy will have waned. Even family relationships, close ones with our spouses and children, must be nurtured or they will starve and grow thin.

3) Assets

We manage our money through budgeting, saving, investing, and protecting what we've accumulated. What about other assets? Maintaining our homes, cars, tools, and clothing are also the responsibility of a manager. When we're careless about managing what we have, items break or wear out more quickly. How long would someone continue to employ a manager who handled his possessions in a slipshod way?

4) Giving and Serving

The good steward doesn't live primarily for himself. Our giving and serving must be managed like everything else. Whatever is in our hands belongs to the Lord and should be used as He would use them. Ephesians 4:25-28 says, *"Let each one of you ... labor, working with his hands what is good, that he may have something to give him who has need."*

The footnote from one of my study Bibles nails it down pretty tight:

> The first motive for a believer to earn money is *that he may have something to give.* The occupational enterprise of Christians is not simply to make a living, but to make possible their being instruments of God's service to mankind through their work and giving.[26]

Whew! That makes it almost *too* clear. Yet imagine the impact! Every believer living comfortably within the abundance God gives them and using the surplus to fulfill His Comprehensive Plan. The Gospel might be spread more effectively. We might even change the world.

Concluding Thought ...

With God's overall purpose in mind—for our world, for us, and for mankind—our motivations and decisions are altered. As manager-stewards of all that God gives us, like Joseph in either Potiphar's house or Pharaoh's palace, we enjoy the privilege of living within the abundance He puts into our hands. Nevertheless, we must never forget that what we manage is not just for us and our children. We must manage everything according to the objectives of the owner.

In the next two chapters, we'll look at the role God has promised to play in our lives. He won't magically take care of everything, but neither does He leave it all up to us. After we've done our part, it's much easier to then rest in trusting God to do His part. Our worries diminish, and the needle on the stress meter moves back into the safety zone.

□ □ □ □ □ _

God's Comprehensive Plan

For Discussion:

- Prior to reading this chapter, did you have an understanding of God's overall plan? What part(s) were missing?

- Can you now state *why* God created mankind? Not just for fellowship, but to do ... what?

- What can you imagine we may "reign" over? Do you suppose God has or will ever create other worlds?

- Discuss the contrast between ownership and management. What have you been owning instead of managing?

- When you consider the extent of your "inventory," what areas are calling most for your attention right now?

What Action Steps Can You Take?

Chapter 5

Know that He Leads & Protects

The steps of a good man are ordered by the LORD
(Psalm 37:23)

From generation to generation, reaching from the prophet, priest, and king to the common man, God has remained engaged in the lives of people. He spoke to them, defended them, and demonstrated His involvement with miracles, exhibiting His presence among them. All those centuries of His involvement were followed up with the greatest miracle of all—He, Himself, became a man. Now, closer than ever, He dwelled among us, teaching and demonstrating how to live, and finally paying the price for our redemption.

After His resurrection, Jesus promised to send the Holy Spirit who would dwell *in* us and guide us into all truth.[27] How much closer, or more involved, could God be? So the question arises, as He lives in us, what is His role? How will He engage in our lives? One clear way to answer that is to look at how Jesus expected the Father to participate in His life.

First, we observe the Holy Spirit *leading* Him. *"Jesus was led up by the Spirit into the wilderness* **to be tempted by the devil***"* (Matthew 4:1, emphasis added). Note that God sometimes may lead you directly into a situation that will prove to be a demanding—and sometimes exasperating time. When He does, be assured it's for your ultimate good, to make you stronger, healthier, wiser.

Second, we see the Father *protecting* Him. On many occasions, Jewish leaders sought to kill Him. *"But no one laid a hand on Him, because His hour had not yet come"* (John 7:30).

Third, we watch God *providing* for Him. Not only did Jesus teach, *"Do not worry about your life, what you will eat or what you will drink; nor about your body, what you will put on"* (Matthew 6:25). We also notice He put that faith into practice. From the time He entered His public ministry He did not work for money, yet the disciples carried around a money box to buy what they needed.[28]

In addition to our observations of how Jesus experienced the Father working in His life, we have the model prayer He taught to His disciples.[29] We commonly refer to this prayer as "The Lord's Prayer." It has been memorized and prayed an untold number of times, and although it's beneficial to repeat the prayer, it's even better to understand its pattern. Within its words, we learn what things we are to ask God for; that is, what we can expect of Him.

The model begins by focusing on God, Himself. We're first and foremost to laud and praise God for all He is and for all He has done: *"Hallowed be Your name."* Nothing lifts our hearts and expectation quite so much as reflecting on Who God is to *us*, and what He has done *for us*. Surely God has done many great things throughout the world, but as we remember to thank Him for the ways He has specifically impacted our lives, our spirits are raised in the expectation that He will continue to be accessible to us, just as He was to Jesus— as "our Father" in heaven.

Let God Show You the Way

The first request uncovered in that prayer is to ask, *"Your kingdom come. Your will be done on earth as it is in heaven."* What does that mean to you? In this segment of your prayers, what specifically are you asking God for?

Let's reflect for a moment on what the kingdom of God is. After John the Baptist was put into prison, the Bible tells us Jesus came into Galilee and preached, *"The kingdom of God is at hand."*[30]   When the Pharisees asked Him when the kingdom of God would come, He answered, *"... the kingdom of God is within you."*[31]

When we pray to the Father that His kingdom would come, we do so with the knowledge that the kingdom already has come and is within us. Now with this understanding, what precisely are we asking for?

Jesus was teaching we are to ask that God's kingdom will invade this world and be further established *through us*. The invasion is accomplished in many ways: witnessing to the world of what God has done in us, going or sending missionaries into all the world, praying for our leaders and against principalities and powers, and in every other way possible conducting ourselves as ambassadors of the Kingdom. When we adjust our mindset to align with His will, applying that thinking to everything we do and manage, the decisions we make will have both His strength and wisdom behind them. It is in this way the Holy Spirit guides His Church. He will always teach and guide us based on the principles of establishing God's kingdom.

Anticipating God's leading is not a matter of waiting for God to tell you to do this or that, turn left or right. Neither an automaton, robot, nor machine can act as ambassador or manager. God wants you to make your own decisions, be in control, and carry responsibility. That's why He created mankind in His own image—to be decision makers. As a son or daughter of God, it is up to you and me to make our own decisions. Nonetheless, we must weigh those choices against whether the results of our decisions will further establish His kingdom.

If you ask God to show you whether you should take this job, or marry that person, it's highly unlikely He'll give a specific directive. Why? Because knowing the principles of His kingdom, and being representatives of that Kingdom, you have the ability to make decisions that are in alignment with His will. Is the decision you're about to make consistent with what you know about God and His will for you? If you aren't sure, seek advice about any part of the decision that's unclear. But in the end, the decision will still be up to you. And often, it's not just a matter of a "yes, it is," or "no, it's not."

God has given you the freedom to make choices; that is, courses of action *you* prefer. As long as those decisions are not in conflict with Kingdom principles, you can freely make choices. Do you want that job? Is that person you love someone who can walk in harmony with you through life? If so, go ahead. It pleases God to give you the desires of your heart, as long as you aren't violating His purpose for your life. Jesus said:

> *"If you then ... know how to give good gifts to your children,*
> *how much more will your Father who is in heaven*
> *give good things to those who ask Him!"*
>
> *(Matthew 7:11)*

It's also important to point out that in addition to not making decisions for us, He also will not provide courage, initiative, or determination. Those things are only achievable by making choices. And that part is up to us. Like Joshua, He wants us to *"be strong and of good courage."* [32] The book of Proverbs also is replete with wise advice which encourages taking the initiative and working at our tasks.

So don't be hesitant. Study and learn the will and purposes of God, and He *will* lead your path. When you make decisions in this way, you'll find yourself doing so without second-guessing yourself or having doubts later, "maybe it wasn't God's will after all."

Our Stronghold and Refuge

Jesus's model for prayer included asking for protection. He told us to pray that we be protected from both ourselves and also the evil one. *"Lead us not into temptation, but deliver us from the evil one."*

The indwelling Holy Spirit, by His very nature, will lead us away from temptation if we heed His prompting. When I'm in a place I don't belong, I know it; I'll bet you do, too. That's not a situation in which I need protection but resolve against my own temptations. If we tolerate unholy suggestions or thoughts, it gives the devil a toehold into our emotions and thinking. So we pray, and using God's power we can overcome.

We can also rest assured that nothing evil can come upon us that doesn't first pass by God's desk. The story of Job illustrates that the tests we encounter may come neither because of our own failings nor initiated by God. Yet no matter what happens, nothing harmful can come our way that He doesn't first allow.

*God is faithful, who will not allow you to be tempted beyond
what you are able, but with the temptation will also make
the way of escape, that you may be able to bear it.*
(1 Corinthians 10:13)

Even at those times we face physical
dangers, God has promised to protect us.
Does He always come to the rescue? I'd like
to say yes, but the answer is apparently, no.
Some questions are hard to answer. For
instance, what about those who are martyred for
Christ? Honestly, I don't know why God allows that.
The Bible talks about special rewards for those who are
martyred, but why he permits such travesties is beyond
my understanding.

In some parts of the world, Christians may die for
their faith. In countries where radical governments and
religious leaders are in control, people must hide their
Christian beliefs and political views. In a number of
countries, people can't step outside their homes without
fear of someone stronger abusing or killing them. Those
people must constantly be on their guard. How
important it is for those of us who enjoy liberty to pray
for fellow believers who are at risk.

In the free world, there are few who face danger.
Those of you who are even allowed to read this book
enjoy a security which much of the world lacks. You can
go almost anywhere, read what you like, believe
whatever you choose, and say what's on your mind.

That, however, doesn't mean you're immune from danger. You, too, must be careful and exercise wisdom. God does not promise to protect the foolish. To conduct yourself with a careless attitude in a dangerous environment, or take unnecessary risk, isn't trusting God; that's being reckless.

When an inadvertent danger enters our lives, we are protected. "*If they* [those that believe] *drink any deadly thing, it shall not hurt them*" (Mark 16:18). And when we are under direct attack, physically or spiritually, God has promised to go with us. He has not, however, promised to keep us out of every battle. In fact, often He wants us in it. But we'll never fight alone.

No one in the Bible saw more real battle time than David. Sometimes he was against what appeared to be insurmountable odds. Not only from Israel's enemy nations, but from the demented King Saul who was obsessed with killing him. Think of the fear that must have flooded his brain. After months of hiding in caves, he looks down from the mountainside and here comes the king with his army to find and kill him. Nevertheless, he writes:

> *"The LORD is my rock and my fortress and my deliverer;*
> *The God of my strength, in whom I will trust;*
> *My shield and the horn of my salvation,*
> *My stronghold and my refuge;*
> *My Savior, You save me from violence."*
>
> *(2 Samuel 22:3)*

What resolute faith! God not only saw him through those confrontations with Saul, but again and again, David had to go to war. After many such battles, David wrote:

> *The LORD is my light and my salvation;*
> *Whom shall I fear?*
> *The LORD is the strength of my life;*
> *Of whom shall I be afraid?*
>
> *(Psalm 27:1)*

What confidence! What absolute joy to rest in the assurance that the strength of Almighty God resides in us and with us.

When it seems like our world is collapsing, when we hear news so devastating that it stops our breath, when faced with a circumstance that seems insurmountable, remember David's words—and his confidence: "*The LORD is the strength of my life; Of whom shall I be afraid?*"

Before leaving this subject, for the sake of debate, let's flip the viewpoint. Is there ever a time God will *not* protect us? Yes, whenever we choose to walk in a direction we know is in violation of those Kingdom principles. It's really quite simple: God walks with those who want to walk with Him. If we decide we'd rather go our own way, He won't oppose us. But, oh, the price we pay for having done so.

It's not easy to own up to our failings, but I must admit that I've chosen my own path too many times. Not infrequently, I found myself uttering a quiet prayer that God would cover my shame and prevent me from being found out. How sad! Often, the biggest price I paid for my wayward behavior was the wasted time, sometimes years, lost in trying to find satisfaction in some other direction.

Concluding Thought ...

God will be a part of our lives just as He was a part of Jesus's life. He will guide and protect as long as we are moving forward in His name and under His banner. When it seems He isn't doing His part, it just gives us away. It means we aren't doing our part. It isn't God who stopped walking with us. It's the other way around.

And, there's more. God's role in our lives is not only to guide and protect, but also to provide for us.

God's Role - Part 1

He Leads and Protects

For Discussion:

- Do you feel confident that God is involved in your life? On what basis?
- In what ways has God led you?
- In what ways have you asked God to decide for you? Do you now believe those choices were really up to you?
- Discuss applying Kingdom Principles to various life situations.
- Jesus repeatedly taught that we are not to worry. In what areas are you most prone to worry? What do you fear?

What Action Steps Can You Take?

-
-
-
-

Chapter 6

Believe that
He Provides

*My God shall supply all your need according to His riches
in glory by Christ Jesus.*

(Philippians 4:19)

Let's continue to follow along the pattern found in the Lord's Prayer. In the next segment, Jesus instructs us to ask God, *"Give us this day our daily bread."*

When we recall the story of Israel coming out of Egypt, nothing stands out more strongly than the promise, *God will provide*. Not only did He provide the manna and quail for food but also water out of rock, clothes that didn't wear out and everything else they needed.

Jesus makes it clear that it's both proper and expected for us to pray for what we need. It isn't begging. Note also that what we need from God isn't just represented by food. We also have need of asking that our debts (sins) be forgiven. Well, aren't they already gone? Yes, yesterday's sins are so far removed that God can't remember them anymore. But until we are made incorruptible by the transformation of our bodies when Christ returns, sin will remain a problem. Make no mistake. Jesus paid the price for *all* sin, past, present, and future. Our daily confession and turning away from our sins, though, is necessary for godliness or holiness.

> *Be renewed in the spirit of your mind ... put on the new man*
> *which was created according to God,*
> *in true righteousness and holiness.*
>
> (Ephesians 4:23-24)

Is there anything God will *not* supply? As long as it's a need, we have His promise that it will *always* be supplied.[33]

Put yourself in God's place by supposing you own a small business. Say you are hiring someone to manage a particular aspect of that business. That manager is working *for* you; that is, for your benefit. If he then comes and says, "Hey boss, I need such and such in order to carry out this job," wouldn't you give him what he needs? After all, if he can't do his job without the material or tool he needs, what's the point of employing him to begin with?

Supplying needs is effortless for God. The Bible says He only needs to speak and things come into existence, even whole worlds! So ask freely. God, like the business owner, wants you to have everything you need to fulfill your ... whoops! ... His purpose.

Why Fear Poverty?

From the previous chapter, we understand that God created us to manage whatever He puts into our hands. That involves relinquishing ownership of everything we handle. Giving up ultimate control, which is reserved for the owner, can be scary. What if we lose our position? What if we get fired? What if...?

Let's think about it. What if we *don't* own "stuff"? First, let's apply the issue to money and physical assets. Managing resources is much more straightforward than discussing how we manage relationships, career, ministry, and other issues. That's why the Bible talks so much about money and assets. Once we get the principle down, we will then better see how it applies to everything under our oversight.

We all carry an innate fear of poverty. Therefore, *choosing* to give up ownership is scary. Without resources, we're vulnerable. No one wants to hear this, but that's just the way God wants you to feel. Not destitute—but dependent. He wants to prove Himself as our Provider, and He wants us to prove ourselves as fully trusting in Him. So, if the question, "What will I do if I don't own things?" grips your mind, that worry bears witness that you are depending on yourself and your own abilities to provide for your needs.

By the way, those feelings are natural. Everybody feels that way. Even though God has promised to always provide, having an abundance of assets gives a sense of security. It's false security, but it reassures us.

Who would have thought it takes only a brief time to wipe out wealth that may have taken a lifetime to acquire? The recent economic downturn in our country has prompted people to joke that their 401k (retirement account) is now a 201 account. Some retirees are once again looking for a job. Even worse, some who overextended themselves because they felt secure stand to lose everything they own.

We learn there is no such thing as security; not with finances, health, relationships, or anything else. The only thing we can trust that will not change is the Lord, Himself. That doesn't suggest that we should go through life with a phobia that our world is likely to end at any time. It does mean, though, it's important to keep things in perspective. We must build as if we're going to live forever, but we must be prepared to accept whatever may happen.

In this context, managing assets that belong to someone else is not nearly so threatening. We don't face the risk of loss; the owner does. And if the owner you work for happens to be *God*—well now! You'll start feeling a lot less worried, as long as you know you've done your part. As the worry dissipates, you'll see that the needle on your stress meter moves back to normal.

Living as a stress-free believer boils down to understanding what God has promised and taking Him at His word. He *will* supply all your needs, according to His riches.

What if you *did* give everything away, and had nothing at all? I've met people who told me they didn't have anything. What they really meant was they didn't own assets of significant monetary value. Although living in poverty in the United States hardly qualifies as "poverty," I realize it's tough, for sure. It's embarrassing, humiliating, and terribly depressing. I think it was Bill Cosby who said that being poor was just one step above being either sick or dead. It's no picnic. Nonetheless, there are two things a believer must keep in mind. First, at least in this country, you don't need to stay in the situation you are currently in. Second, and more to the point of this discussion, you may not possess much, but remember that it's God's plan for you to *own* nothing at all. It belongs to Him.

Does that mean God wants us to be poor; or give away everything and live like a pauper? Not even close. The very opposite of poverty is God's plan for you. He wants you to have abundance and has promised to increase your assets as you increase in your ability to manage them. The only person in the whole Bible to whom Jesus ever told to give everything away was that rich young ruler. And it wasn't to impoverish him but to illustrate a reality: the young man's assets owned him!

Let's turn it around. Can we then say that God wants us to be rich? How much wealth we are to hold and how much to give away will be dealt with at greater length in the final chapter. For now, let's make this point clear: God is looking for "good" stewards. That is, those who can manage ever-increasing spheres of assets and responsibility while relinquishing ownership.

How much we *hold* has nothing to do with *our* wealth. It's impossible for you and me to ever become rich—or poor. All assets belong to the Lord. What matters to the Master is the degree to which He can trust us, not only with assets we now hold but with even more. Managing ever-increasing assets stands as proof to both our ability and reliability (providing, of course, we manage those assets in His behalf).

Enough is Never an Issue

God has promised to always provide. Yet our nerves continue to yank at us, "What if we don't have enough?" That nagging fear is as old as history. From the very beginning, even in the Garden of Eden, mankind has feared not having enough. What were Adam and Eve tempted to think? "If you eat this fruit, *then* ...." Then what? They had everything they needed yet came to fear they were being held back, limited, and deprived. Of what? In their case, knowledge.

Regardless of how much you will have in any arena, the temptation is to fear it won't be enough or that you're being deprived of your fair share. "What if I don't have enough money? Enough health? What if I run out of time, am not smart enough, not well connected enough, am not sufficiently accepted... ?" *ad infinitum*. Oh yes, here's one more: "What if the world is passing me by and others are having more fun or getting more benefits than I am?"

Remember this: Recurring thoughts of "not having enough" propagate fear. Do you recall this axiom from the beginning of this book?

> *Stress causes worry, worry creates fear, and fear is the opposite of faith. When we worry, we're not trusting God. It's a signal that we're afraid; we fear He won't come through for us.*

Closely related to the fear of not having enough is the intense desire for more. More of what? Everything! How much more? A limitless amount. Money, toys, experiences, pleasure, power, authority, and the list can go on. Greed is motivated by the desire to indulge, to consume, to intensify pleasure. It is the substance of gluttony.

Even very wealthy people fear not having enough. While in San Diego, I was working with several trust officers of a major bank. One day we met with one of their clients, a wealthy widow whose net worth was over ten million dollars. She was 80 years old, living very modestly but still was afraid she would run out of money. "I don't want to end up in a nursing home," she said.

It made me smile when one of the men tried to assure her: "Honey, you don't have to worry. You could *buy* a nursing home! Two if you want." Do you think that assuaged her fears? Nope.

I've met with people who have more money than they will ever need but fear they either don't or won't have enough. Most of us think if we just had a little more wealth, the stress would go away. I assure you, it will not.

Let's Not Forget

Jesus confronted the "it may not be enough" fear several times. Possibly the most vivid example was what took place after He fed the loaves and fish to the multitude. The entire story can be reviewed in Mark, chapter eight.

He fed over 4,000 people with only seven loaves of bread and a few small fish. They then had seven baskets of fragments left over. The focal teaching point to His disciples took place right *after* that miracle.

They entered a boat, now traveling to the other side of the lake. He began teaching them to beware of the yeast of the Pharisees. Immediately, they felt guilty because they'd only brought a single loaf of bread onto the boat. They began "reasoning" about this. In all likelihood they were blaming each other for forgetting to bring more bread.

As soon as Jesus realized the topic of their discussion, He expressed His frustration: "Why are you talking about *bread?*" He then reminded them of the two miracles they had witnessed which had to do with bread. (The first was the feeding of the 5,000, recorded in Mark chapter six, and now this most recent feeding of 4,000.)

Now, after having witnessed all that, here they sat worrying about whether they would have enough to eat! Can you imagine His frustration? What else must He do to make them see? Thirteen men in a boat *with Jesus* and a full loaf of bread to share and they were worried they might not have enough. How could this be? What more would it take to get them to understand that providing *whatever* is needed is simply not a matter of concern to God?

As we review this story, their continued lack of faith may seem unreasonable, even comical, but let's be a bit easy on them. It's not a simple lesson to learn. Just like us, these men were adults who'd spent their entire lives thinking only of providing for themselves. As likely as not, they'd been taught they'd have to fight for everything they'd receive. Trusting that God would provide, day-by-day, just didn't make sense. It's contrary to the way our world thinks. But consequently, it's the touchstone to which our own thinking reverts, especially during a setback.

God Opens Doors

Trusting an invisible God for provision may seem scary, even crazy, but testimonies of His reliability abound. Ask and you'll find a multitude of people who will testify, "He's never yet failed me." And I, for one, would volunteer to stand at the front of that line to tell what He's done for me.

My current ministry serves as an example. Believing the Lord was leading me to share with believers what I'd learned about finance and gift planning, I launched out into a new ministry without financial backing. Very few pastors knew or remembered me, as I'd been inactive in ministry for almost 20 years.

While visiting in Southern California, someone told me of a large church in the area. By instinct (or could it be the prompting of the Holy Spirit), I called and asked the executive pastor if I could stop and introduce myself. Although he had an upcoming appointment and could only give me about fifteen minutes, he agreed.

I explained what I was doing and asked if maybe I could come as a guest speaker for a midweek service. He asked me to wait as he went to see the senior pastor. Although I'd never met him, the senior pastor knew of me from my past ministry and sent word that he'd like me to address the entire congregation (of several thousand people) during a regular worship service. Surprised as we were, the executive pastor and I had a date set up.

One reason I'm sharing this story is to illustrate that God often meets your need at the same time as meeting that of someone else. The speaking engagement certainly met my need. I was yet unknown, but ministering in such a large church opened many other doors. The church's generous honorarium also helped me financially. And the benefit to the church and its members turned out to be substantial.

For the next two days following my speaking engagement, I met with people in 30-minute appointments, helping many of them create their first legal will. Using software I carry with me, I helped them enter the data and printed out the document. Many of those people expressed gratitude and said they were so pleased to have at least a first step in an estate plan. So here, the individual members received help.

As people use the software, one question asked is if they would like to leave a bequest to any charities they support. Without my input, quite a few of them responded, "Oh, yes. We hadn't thought of that before, but we'd like to leave something to support our church." Bequests were made to other charitable organizations as well, but the most common gift for the church was 10%

of their estate—probably based on the practice of giving the tithe.

The resulting benefit for the church is that 77 new wills were created. Almost $600,000 was committed to the ongoing ministry of the church and almost an equal amount to other charities, most of which were Christian ministries. Neither I, nor any of the pastors, asked people to include charitable gifts. The desire to do so already resided in their hearts.

What a joy! As I believe I acted on His prompting, the Lord provided not only for my need, but that of 77 people and the support of the future ministries of their church. Most of such impressive funding won't be realized for 15 or 20 years, but it will guarantee that the ministry those people have invested in during their lifetimes will continue to produce spiritual fruit.

Concluding Thought ...

When understood from God's standpoint, we see that He cannot assign greater areas of responsibility to a manager who is focused on hoarding assets into his or her own private stash. In the final chapter, we'll focus on specific things we now hold in our hands: how we manage our family, our career, our finances, and so on. But first, we must ask ourselves: Have we let go of the ownership which interferes with good management?

One of our most natural instincts is to claim as much ownership as possible. Even toddlers are quick to announce "Mine!" whether they own it or not. That's an instinct. It's part of our natural character. It represents our Dark-side thinking. Once freed from the role of ownership, we become better prepared for the role of management.

As we consider living "stress-free," can you see how trusting God to fulfill His role in our lives relieves tremendous pressure? Sure, we'll have to remind ourselves time and again of His promises and faithfulness, but as we bring those things to mind the stress meter goes back to black.

God's Role - Part 2

He Provides

For Discussion:

- Can you share a time when you were convinced that God provided for some need in your life?
- In which areas are you sometimes apprehensive, afraid that maybe He won't show up in time?
- Have you felt that having just a little more money would make you feel secure? Do you still think so?
- Have you wondered if God wanted you to be rich? Or give everything to the poor?
- Suggest ways that God provides for us other than money. Is there an area where you are now trusting Him for provision?

What Action Steps Can You Take?

-
-
-
-

Part 2 - God's Role

Let's Summarize:

From before the first day of creation, God had a plan.

Although our current lifespan is measured in years, God's intent for you is to live and partner with Him forever.

It's impossible for us to grasp the scope of an infinite God who is not flesh. The Bible teaches us that He is spirit, present everywhere, and all powerful. How could we wrap our minds around that? Well, we can't. By coming to understand Him and His plan through the Scripture and the life of Jesus, however, we can understand what God's comprehensive plan is for us.

Only He had the capacity to provide a way out of the Darkness brought on by sin. When we choose to receive His free gift of salvation, He not only forgives our sins but also—in some miraculous way—allows His Spirit to live within us. He's not only active in our world, He personally resides within us. What an incredible, wonderful, and humbling reality.

Now He invites us to partner with Him in that comprehensive plan. Although He owns the world and everything in it, He's invited us to work as His representatives in managing every part of it: the commerce, relationships with one another, and even announcing the Good News of His plan to the world of people that remain in the Dark.

We each have a role to fulfill. The effectiveness of accomplishing God's plan in our world is largely dependent upon how well we develop and mature as His sons and daughters. Yet it's not all up to us, for God has a role as well. He's promised to lead us, protect us, and provide whatever is needed for us to become all we can be.

When this life is over, that's just the beginning of the eternal phase of our life with God. Jesus said:

"Let not your heart be troubled; you believe in God,
believe also in Me. In My Father's house are many mansions;
if it were not so, I would have told you. I go to prepare
a place for you. And if I go and prepare a place for you,
I will come again and receive you to Myself; that where I am,
there you may be also."

(John 14:1-3)

God's role is to provide all that we need to accomplish His master plan. Therefore, don't let your heart be troubled. No matter where you go or what your assignment may be, God will fulfill His role by remaining active in your life and seeing you through anything that comes your way.

Part Three

The Believer's Role

Overview

In this last section of the book, we move the spotlight from God's role in our lives to the roles He designed mankind to fulfill.

Understanding God's comprehensive plan, and that He walks along with us through every step of our lives, gives us the assurance we need to now address our roles without the pressure of having to "perform." He holds no desire for us to try to impress Him. Nor are we in competition with anyone else. With that in mind, we now look more closely at the two roles we are to fulfill.

First, wherever we go, we represent Him; that is, we are His ambassadors. The second role is to manage and develop all that He puts under our oversight. The Bible refers to this second role as being stewards. As we are faithful over what's already been given, more will be added. Living as stress-free believers involves handling not only physical assets but also our relationships and ministry responsibilities.

Chapter 7

You Are Ambassadors

"Go therefore and make disciples of all the nations,
baptizing them in the name of the Father and of the Son
and of the Holy Spirit, teaching them to observe all things
that I have commanded you; and lo, I am with you always,
even to the end of the age."

(Matthew 28:19-20)

Jesus appeared for the last time on earth to an assembly of people just before His ascension.[34] According to the Gospel of Matthew, He spoke to his eleven remaining disciples in private prior to being taken back up to heaven. His last words are recorded (in the above passage) in what we now refer to as the Great Commission.

Starting from the city of Jerusalem in that small nation of Israel, the Gospel has spread and been preached all over the world. Churches will continue to send missionaries to those who have not yet heard, but the Great Commission is not fulfilled by missionaries alone. Those words of Jesus, as well as the promise of the empowering Holy Spirit, are addressed to you, and to me, and to *"as many as the Lord our God will call."*[35]

Going to all nations includes the nation in which we live. Sadly, there are many all around us who have never heard the good news of Jesus Christ. Oh sure, most have heard His name and know about Christianity, but many may never have had a conversation with a genuinely born-again Christian. How can they learn if those of us who have found new life in Christ don't tell them of our experience?

Kingdom Representatives

If you've been a Christian for very long, you've undoubtedly learned that we should be witnesses, leading people to Christ and bringing people to church. How do you feel about that? Maybe even guilty that you aren't doing it? In this chapter, we'll take a closer look at ways to become a more effective witness and one who disciples others. Before attempting to lead others to Christ, it will help to consider the role we are being asked to fulfill.

An ambassador is a formal representative of a ruling authority, sent from his host country to another country. Jesus explained that we are no longer of this world but now are members of God's kingdom.[36] Wherever we now go in this world, our former home, we go as representatives (citizens) of God's kingdom; that is, we are ambassadors.

Let's review how an ambassador is chosen. He is first of all a reliable citizen; that is, one who always represents his country, standing up for its values without apology, being careful never to bring embarrassment or reproach on those he speaks in behalf of. Ambassadors are chosen carefully. He or she must not only understand the country's laws but also the principles that govern it. Let's pause here for a moment to point out a disparity in terms.

Acting as a witness and serving as a representative are separate behaviors. Anyone can act as a witness, and certainly an ambassador must exemplify that role. To be trusted with being the spokesman for a nation, however, requires a much higher skill level than that of simply witnessing. The man who serves in the role of ambassador must be an expert regarding his country and its government. He must also be articulate, having the ability to weigh his words carefully. To speak carelessly, or misrepresent those in whose stead he stands, can cause havoc.

In order to fulfill the mandate we call the Great Commission, we must commit to *becoming* ambassadors. No person can have that ability simply by obtaining citizenship. What that means for you and me as believers is that we must be *on the road* to learning and acquiring the skills needed for that position. Being en route includes expanding both our knowledge and ability:

1) Knowledge by the continuous study of God's Word, His kingdom, and the principles involved.

2) Ability by adding the skills of learning to speak accurately and effectively.

Dedicating time and energy toward both of those efforts gets us well on the road to qualifying as ambassadors.

Living in a way that exemplifies Christian values fulfills Jesus's command to *"Let your light so shine before men, that they may see your good works and glorify your Father in heaven."* [37] That, by itself, is a great testimony. Getting to that stage, however, is a process. It sometimes takes months to walk away from the patterns of life we acquired from years of walking in Darkness. Better give yourself, and those around you, a bit of leeway and time to grow in Christ.

As you mature in your faith, one day you'll go beyond the role of just witnessing regarding your experiences. More and more, you'll become an ambassador. In the meantime, as part of your preparation for that prestigious role, you're to be both a witness and disciple maker.

Eye Witnesses

Review the Great Commission at the beginning of this chapter and you'll see that what we're to do (in contrast to what we're to be, as ambassadors), is to lead people to salvation and then train them. First we lead them to the point of asking Jesus into their hearts, followed by water baptism which gives public testimony of that faith. After that, the training toward discipleship begins.

First things, first. How do we effectively witness to people?

Did you ever ask yourself what a witness does? A witness is someone who gives testimony to what he or she has seen, heard, or experienced. And that's it! Visualize a court of law. You're seated in the back row watching a trial, and a witness is called. The witness begins to recall what he or she heard someone else say. "Objection!" the attorney calls out.

That testimony will not be allowed. Why? Because it isn't what the witness saw, heard, or experienced, personally. A witness can only testify from firsthand experience. That's the only thing considered as evidence. A witness is not allowed to argue the case, speculate, or give his or her opinion about anything.

Who then argues the case for either the prosecution or defense? Answer: the attorneys. It's their job to first of all extract the evidence in the case, and then convince the judge or jury of the truth the evidence has proven. Now apply this to witnessing of your spiritual experience.

When you testify to someone, it's vital for you not to step into the role of an advocate. The job of convincing and pressing the point home is for the attorney to carry out. In our application, that's the Holy Spirit. It is up to Him to convict the world of sin, righteousness, and judgment.[38] Very few have come to Christ because of a persuasive argument. Repentance comes from what's in the heart, not the head. When we talk to others about what God has done for us and in us, the Holy Spirit uses that evidence to prove the truth of the case. After coming to faith, when we hide our Christian life, the Holy Spirit doesn't have evidence to work with.

What does good witnessing look like? It's the truth, the whole truth, and nothing but the truth about what you have experienced. Good witnessing is simply telling what you know, without holding back. It doesn't matter if people believe you. If they scoff in unbelief, just shrug your shoulders. "Hey, that's what happened to me." And go on your way.

Our hesitancy to give our testimony to unbelievers is often based on fear that we either don't know what to say or that we'll be cornered in an argument we won't know how to defend. If we restrict our words to testifying as a witness, avoiding those of an advocate, what we fear will never happen.

Think about that for a moment. Can you share about what you've experienced? Of course you can. It may not be eloquent, but you're just telling the truth. A court of law never indicts a witness for inarticulate language. If the testimony is confusing or not clear, it's up to the attorney to keep probing.

What if someone finds your experience unbelievable and asks you how that could possibly be? The answer is an easy one: "I don't know." If you don't know, just say so. Your job at that point is not to teach, preach, or defend. Your job is ... well, you now know what it is. Right?

As time goes by, and you've had time to study the Bible and discuss various points with other believers and teachers, you'll gain the ability to answer honest questions from unbelievers. When asked how being born again is possible, you'll be able to explain it. Eventually, you'll become a teacher—at least of sorts. Depending on God's gifts to you, you may become very capable in one area or another. You'll also gain enough experience to know when the question is not legitimate or heartfelt.

Dodging those situations is as easy as saying, "That's beyond me." Don't let an antagonist lure you into an argument. If you succumb, you'll be taken out of your most effective role as a witness. Irrespective of how fast you qualify as an ambassador, you can be a witness—even right now.

There's one more point I'd like to make here that I think is important. People may resent our message, doubt our testimony, or even become hostile. When that happens, please be patient with those people. Remember that those who are blind *cannot* understand the Light you speak about. They are not yet citizens of our new Kingdom-nation and won't understand its culture. To them, it's a foreign country and a foreign language.

If people can feel that you love and truly care about them, they'll be much more open to considering the honesty of what you say. Ask yourself about your motives when you talk to someone about your faith. If your objective is to convince them that their way of living is sinful, that your thinking is right and theirs wrong, or that you're trying to capture them as a member of your church, don't you think they'll resent that? Wouldn't you?

If, on the other hand, you demonstrate that you understand why they live the way they do, but that you've discovered a new way of living that's brought you a surprising joy, how can that be offensive? They may not buy into it, but convincing them isn't your role.

The Gift of Evangelist

In this chapter, we're addressing the role of every believer in becoming fully equipped ambassadors. The road to fulfilling that role begins with learning to share what God has done for us with others. What about door-to-door witnessing, street meetings, passing out tracts, and other evangelistic efforts? We are taught that God gives unique and individual gifts to each person:

> *Now concerning spiritual gifts, brethren, I do not want you to be ignorant ... There are diversities of gifts, but the same Spirit. There are differences of ministries, but the same Lord. And there are diversities of activities, but it is the same God who works all in all ... But one and the same Spirit works all these things, distributing to each one individually as He wills.*
>
> (1 Corinthians 12:1-11)

All of us may participate in the above mentioned evangelistic efforts. Within our community, we can raise an awareness of our church, reach out to those in need, and find ways of becoming "salt and light" to our world. The gift of evangelism, however, is something that God gives to certain individuals, just as he does the gift of pastor or teacher. Supporting those God raises up to these offices strengthens the church, helps to carry out the Great Commission, and keeps us safe from error.

Inviting Unbelievers to Church

What about bringing our unsaved friends to church? In many churches, members are reminded frequently to witness to friends and colleagues and invite them to church. Why? Of course, we want them to get saved. The general thought behind the encouragement is if we invite people to the services, and while there they respond to an appeal to accept Christ ... Wonderful! A new soul is reborn and the church will grow. And although that may be true, it's important to remember that the church is a *gathering of believers*. Some have concluded that inviting others to church is witnessing. It isn't.

Unbelievers attend a church service for a variety of reasons: the urging of a friend, a special event, to see a Christmas play, or whatever. Either out of courtesy to a friend or curiosity about the event, they become willing to enter this "private club" of believers, of which they are starkly aware they don't belong. It's in that setting, we hope and pray that the Holy Spirit will give them courage to take action and decide to begin their life of following Jesus.

There's no doubt that many make their first profession of faith in church services. I know I did. But,the decision to open one's heart, repent of sin, and call upon God is the concluding result of the witnessing of the believer and subsequent conviction of the Holy Spirit. It is *not* dependent upon being in church. The conviction comes about during times of personal reflection after hearing the testimony (or witness) of someone whose life has been changed. The gestation period may be days, months, or years, but the seed eventually ripens. The action of then calling on God for salvation may take place anywhere: at home, watching television, at the invitation of a friend to pray together, or in church.

Now why is this important to think about and discuss? As followers of Christ, each of us desire to become effective at witnessing and discipling others. Too often, we feel clumsy and ill-equipped to ask the question, "Would you like to ask God to come into your life, right now?" That's a confrontational question. We don't want to be rude or embarrass the other person. And we also don't want to behave in a way that labels us as a religious nut. Yet our heart, our conscience, and the Holy Spirit all seem to tug at us to reach out to those who need salvation.

Inviting people in an environment where an appeal might be presented can be important. But we must learn to become comfortable asking the confrontational question, "Would you like to? Right now?" Can we proceed without holding back in order to ask them to church to avoid dealing with it ourselves?

How do we gain enough confidence to one day ask someone if they'd like to invite Christ into their lives?

Inviting Unbelievers to Step Into the Light

Getting comfortable first with telling the truth, the whole truth, and nothing but the truth is the first step. Not preaching, putting the finger on someone, or even prematurely asking them to become a Christian. Just living as a believer and letting others know that you've committed your life in a new direction. Answer their questions. Tell them what you know. Admit what you don't know.

In my view, the greatest mistake in witnessing that I've seen is when people attempt to lead someone to Jesus when a relationship that would make such a "confrontation" appropriate hasn't yet been established. Asking someone you barely know a personal question about making a decision to repent of their sins would be akin to asking them to reveal details about their personal finances or relationship with their spouse. It's simply out of line.

Live your life around others as a Christian. Just be what you claim to be. If you mess up in front of them, like cursing when you slam your knee against the desk, acknowledge it. "Whoops! Sorry. Still working on that language problem."

You'll never live a spotless life. Don't pretend that you do. That's not "the whole truth."

If you'd like to read your Bible at work during your lunch hour, that's great. Do it. But do it privately. If you're doing it as a show, instead of your personal conviction, that's not truthful. People will pick up on that right away. If you're using your Bible as a calling card, don't be surprised if people avoid you in the same way you would avoid a salesman who's passing out his business card, just waiting for eye contact so he can launch into his spiel. Jesus said that when you do a charitable deed, fast, or pray, do so in secret and not before men.[39] The principle, again, is one of candor. Our witness becomes more effective when we are completely honest.

Witnessing has its greatest effect upon those with whom we have first established a relationship. Think of the people who first witnessed to you. I mean those who had a real affect on you. Were they strangers? Casual acquaintances? In all likelihood, they were friends or family, people you trust at some level. The bottom line to effective witnessing is to be friends with people. Be genuinely interested in them, not in what you can get from them. Love them.

When the time seems right with someone you've testified to, then ask the question: "Would you like to ask Him in? Right now?"

Maybe the answer will be "No." Well, OK, it was just a question. Accept the answer. You aren't a failure and haven't done anything wrong. It's no more complicated than asking someone if they'd like a cup of coffee. "No? OK, I was just asking." If you learn to ask the question casually, the other person also avoids embarrassment. When they're ready, either they or the Holy Spirit will let you know. Be careful not to beat up on people because of your eagerness or compassion for their soul. That may only end up severing a good relationship and end the possibility of your "being there" at the right time.

John Amstutz makes the point very well:

> Good works may need to precede and prepare the soil for the communication of the good news of the gospel. As has been said, "People do not care how much you know until they know how much you care." The communication of the good news of the kingdom is in word and deed.[40]

Training New Converts/Believers

After witnessing and leading people to faith, the second step—that of making disciples—is *"teaching them to observe all things that I have commanded you."* That responsibility is not just yours alone, it's the role of the church. It's done together, in cooperation with other mature believers.

The Church, in its simplest form, is the gathering together of believers. Whenever two or more assemble in His name, Jesus has promised to be in their midst.[41] In that assembly, together we worship, pray, provide instruction, discuss, and so on. In the process of that interaction, discipleship takes place. We learn, grow, are corrected, trained, and become stronger and more mature.

The Apostle Paul explained that Jesus gave His Church special gifts,

> *For the equipping of the saints for the work of ministry,*
> *for the edifying of the body of Christ, till we all come*
> *to the unity of the faith and of the knowledge*
> *of the Son of God, to a perfect man, to the measure*
> *of the stature of the fullness of Christ; that we should*
> *no longer be children, tossed to and fro and carried about*
> *with every wind of doctrine, by the trickery of men,*
> *in the cunning craftiness of deceitful plotting,*
> *but, speaking the truth in love, may grow up in all things*
> *into Him who is the head—Christ.*
>
> (Ephesians 4:13-15)

As we gather with other believers, we each learn from one another by sharing our experiences and difficulties. The teaching, pastoring, prophetic and other ministries, moreover, are special gifts that God raises up within our assemblies. The purpose of those gifts is *"for the equipping of the saints and edifying of the body of Christ."* [42]

Before you join into the effort of making disciples, it's important to give sufficient time to becoming a disciple, yourself. That means being a learner, a student, one who is open to new thought, and to correction.

Attending not only general worship services but Sunday school classes, sanctioned home group meetings, and structured Bible studies work together to prevent us from falling into error. Our minds are sharpened as we enter into discussions on why each book of the Bible was written, the history and makeup of culture, and how to deal with verses that appear to conflict with each other. In other words, we must *prepare* ourselves to teach others, just as Paul encouraged Timothy:

> *Be diligent to present yourself approved to God,*
> *a worker who does not need to be ashamed,*
> *rightly dividing the word of truth.*
>
> (2 Timothy 2:15)

The importance of gathering together as believers cannot be overemphasized.[43] As is true in every walk of life, it's through our involvement that we move from ignorance to knowledge, from novice to veteran, from apprenticeship to masters. Don't be too eager. Stepping into the role of a teacher without the sanction and ordaining of church elders can be disastrous. As James 3:1 cautions, *"Let not many of you become teachers, knowing that we shall receive a stricter judgment."*

A significant portion of the New Testament is made up of letters written to correcting problems that arose in the early church from people who *were* too eager. People started teaching before they'd been sufficiently trained.

When the same thing happens, well-intentioned people can easily fall into error.

Concluding Thought ...

Every believer should practice and become comfortable sharing his or her testimony with others. Similarly, every believer must become a disciple and encourage others to do the same. In this way, we teach, strengthen, and inspire each other. On the other hand, it's important to distinguish between witnessing, teaching, and preaching. If we begin preaching in our attempts to witness, our audience may decide to quit the "performance."

In addition to our commission as ambassadors of the Kingdom of God, we've been called as stewards or managers. In the remaining chapters, we'll talk about how we're to function in that role. The principles of management will be the same for us all, but the skills needed to manage what God gives to us individually will differ. So first, let's consider the principles we must all embrace.

You may even be surprised to learn that you must qualify to serve as a manager. Not everyone, you see, is eligible. At least not yet.

The Believer's Role

As Ambassadors

For Discussion:

- ☻ Talk about your idea of an ambassador. Are there any you know of and admire? Why?

- ☻ If you were president and selecting an ambassador, what qualifications would you look for? Are any of those qualities missing in your life as a believer?

- ☻ Do you feel awkward about witnessing? Can you share your testimony with believers? Can you talk about *your* faith at all, without feeling clumsy?

- ☻ In what ways do you feel you could help disciple newer believers? Who was most effective in discipling you?

What Action Steps Can You Take?

- ☻
- ☻
- ☻
- ☻

Chapter 8

You Are Managers

Management is doing things right;
leadership is doing the right things.
-- Peter Drucker

Jesus made it clear that God's intent is for us to profitably manage whatever is in our hands. The two Scripture sections that underscore this teaching are The Parable of the Ten Minas and The Parable of the Talents, both of which pertain to amounts of money in New Testament times. More accurately, these are the stories of good and bad managers.

The entire stories can be read in Luke 19:11-27, and in Matthew 25:14-30. In both tales, the servants who did not use what the master had given them were rebuked and had their money taken away. Those who managed their assets well were rewarded. Matthew 25:21 reads:

> *"Well done, good and faithful servant; you were faithful*
> *over a few things, I will make you ruler over many things.*
> *Enter into the joy of your lord."*

The above verse conveys a principle which will govern your life both now and eternally. In any area of your life, if you're faithful and diligent in managing what you have, you'll see an increase. That's God's promise to you. It's not a speculation.

This principle of good management is most clearly demonstrated in the area of money or asset management. Maybe that's why Jesus used these parables and why the Bible has so many references to managing money. Dr. Kenneth Ulmer, in his book *Making Your Money Count*, points out that in both of the above parables, the command of the master was to "do business" until Jesus returns. He explains further:

> The phrase in Greek means to do the activity of a trader or a banker. So here we have Jesus giving the disciples instructions to perform a task that at first glance doesn't appear all that spiritual. This is significant. Everything we do is within our spiritual relationship to God, but not all we do is necessarily spiritual in nature. In other words, we must still live in, dwell in and be a part of this world. There is no separation for us between the sacred and the secular —it's all lumped into life.[44]

Learning to manage *everything* God puts into our hands extends beyond handling money. We also must manage our relationships, vocations, and every other task, many of which may not seem connected to the spiritual side of life.

In their enthusiasm to draw closer to God, some believers fail to connect the importance of balancing the management of the spiritual and practical sides of life. Not long ago, I addressed this topic while speaking at a large church in California. During the course of my message, I pointed out that in those areas of life in which you continue to struggle and keep coming up empty, it's a sure sign you haven't yet learned to manage what you already have, *in that area*.

After the service, several people came up to greet and chat with me. One lady, probably in her fifties, held back until the crowd had cleared. "I want to challenge you on a point you made in your sermon," she said. She went on to insist there had to be a flaw in the theology of what her pastors and I were telling her. From her childhood she had been taught to manage money well. Yet she now had lost virtually everything. The principle and the results just didn't line up. From her point of view, she'd been doing everything correctly and yet God wasn't coming through on His end.

Whether or not she had managed well or poorly is something neither I nor her pastors could possibly know. What we do know is that Jesus *promised* if we were faithful over a little, He would make us masters over much.[45]

It's always wise to evaluate our decisions, our actions, and the results. How else can we determine if we are being effective, mistaken, or have been careless? And when we've done what we know to do and the results are lacking, it's time to get further input on what we don't yet understand.

It's also necessary to realize that sometimes bad things happen to good people. It's not a matter of God punishing us; we just need to grow stronger in a given area. There's no answer to why people get sick, die young, lose jobs, or even get struck by lightning. Disasters and tragedies happen around the world to good and bad people, even to God's sons and daughters. Jesus said that God *"makes His sun rise on the evil and on the good, and sends rain on the just and on the unjust."*[46]

Regardless of where you are in life, the principle is to manage whatever is in your hands right now. Maybe you're someone who has "lost everything." OK, but look around. What remains? Get over the grief and manage what's left. The same is true if you've gone through a divorce, have a terminal illness, broke the law and are facing punishment, or any other travesty that may have come your way.

Not long ago, I was talking to a professional counselor who told me about an older married couple she'd counseled. They apparently were at wits' end with one another. "We have nothing in common anymore." They both agreed on that point. The counselor then listened while each spouse launched into a diatribe about how hard it was to live with their unreasonable mate.

"Don't you have *anything* you still enjoy together?" she asked.

"No!" the husband insisted. After a moment to reflect he added, "Except for about 15 minutes of peace after dinner each night."

"Well, there you are," said my friend. "That's a starting point. Just go with that!"

Her advice sounded so funny to me that I laughed out loud. Absolutely nothing to work with and only a scant 15 minutes of peace. But my friend is no dummy. She saw the first building block of what it would take to start rebuilding that which had been torn down. I suppose that couple had a lot of work to do together, but all was not lost. They still had 15 minutes. And from that we learn a most important lesson: *all is never lost.*

Remember the adage, "What is, is." You'll never gain ground by reflecting on what used to be or by harboring hard feelings about the past. There are tragedies in life worth crying and mourning over, but limit that crying and mourning to a restricted season. Then, once again, you'll find yourself back in the only position God ever created you for—manager of what is, right now.

Qualifying for Management

The owner of every business looks for both of these qualifications in any manager: the ability to do the right things and the determination to carry them out. What, exactly, are those "right things"?

The two requisites for managing God's assets are set forth in the book of Exodus: trust and obedience. In this account, God sets before His people a pattern of what's required for them to enter into and then possess their Promised Land. It was not a simple matter of "packing up and getting there." They needed to develop new competencies to manage what would be given them.

For 430 years these descendants of Abraham had lived in the northern region of Egypt known as Goshen. This is part of the Nile Delta and is rich with water and fertile land.

Then, 300 years after Joseph's time, their fortunes changed. In about 1500 BCE the Egyptian rulers turned against people who had come from other countries: this included the Israelites. They became slaves and had to work for others rather than for themselves.[47]

It was during this time that Moses grew up in the palace of Pharaoh, never forgetting he was Jewish. After killing an Egyptian for abusing a Jewish slave, he fled

Egypt and lived in the Sinai Peninsula until God called him to return and lead His people out from slavery.

The book of Exodus records the story of Israel moving out of Egypt and into Canaan. Exodus, which means *way out*, tells of the Israelites' escape, their travel to Mt. Sinai, the giving of the Ten Commandments, and many lessons demonstrating how to live a life of faith and purpose.

> The Book of Exodus is the story of two covenant partners—God and Israel. Exodus sets forth in narrative form how Israel became the people of Yahweh and lays out the covenant terms by which the nation was to live as God's people.[48]

The first portion of the book begins with the story of the deliverance of Israel from the hand of Pharaoh, concluding with the crossing of the Red Sea. Immediately following that crossing, God makes known the first of two prerequisites of what it will take to partner with Him and release His favor.

We need to pay close attention here, because both of these prerequisites are still valid today. Before we can qualify as those who manage God's assets, we must learn to trust and then obey.

The First Requisite: Trust

For generations, the only life these people had known was one of slavery. They couldn't rely on anything. Everyday, their future depended on the whim of their master or his aides. They were not allowed to think for themselves or make plans. Nonetheless, they knew their history: God had promised them a land which would one day belong to them.

Keep this in mind: They were well aware of both their destiny and their destination as a people. They weren't just leaving Egypt. They were en route to a specific place on the map. These were the "children of Israel," descendants of Abraham, Isaac, and Jacob (whose name had been changed to Israel). The land had been promised to their forefathers and now they were setting out to claim it. Hallelujah!

Every man, woman, and child over the age of eight knew where that land was. Just to the north of Egypt is the Mediterranean Sea. Follow the road directly east and you end up at the Promised Land. No mystery, nothing convoluted. By taking the direct route, the trip comprised 250 miles or about a month's journey. What an exciting prospect that must have been. Exodus 13:17-22, however, recounts:

When Pharaoh had let the people go ...
God did not lead them by [the] way ... that was near;
... God led the people around by way of the wilderness....
And the LORD went before them by day
in a pillar of cloud ... and by night in a pillar of fire....

For the next forty years, God would lead them by day and night—both *where* and *when* He wanted them to go. Sometimes the pillar of cloud or fire would move or stop for just a day or so. Sometimes it would remain for months. The people were to remain alert and follow God's lead.

As long as they were moving directly toward their destination, I doubt if anybody spoke a dissenting word. When those pillars started moving in the opposite direction, *south*, toward what we now refer to as Mt. Sinai, I imagine lots of voices could be heard. How frustrating! Undoubtedly, they still felt vulnerable and unprotected out in the dessert by themselves, lacking any kind of trained military protection.

It's here, however, where they learn the first essential conduct of managers: trusting God to direct their future. *He* would lead *them*, not the other way around.

The message was this: as long as the pillar doesn't move—stay put! And when it does move, set your apprehensions and inconvenience aside and start packing. Can you hear the message? If God doesn't open a door, speak to or lead you in some specific way, stay put until He does. And when He does, trust Him and get ready.

How does it apply to us today? Coming to grips with how much we can count on God to specifically lead us can be difficult, if not awkward. So let's look deeper to clear our thinking on this.

In my many years of being around Christians, I've come to realize that it's uncommon for God to give direct orders to do this or that, go here or there. Some people, on the other hand, testify that God gave direction with such lucidity that all ambiguity was dispelled. This kind of testimony, however, appears to be much more unusual than is common for most Christian—even strong leaders. Seldom will God tell you which job to take, where to attend college, or who to marry. A much more common experience is for God to lead you in your thinking, unlike giving orders to an android.

We no longer have a pillar of cloud or fire to follow. It's no longer that elementary. God continues to lead but with a resource far superior to a pillar of fire or cloud. Jesus promised that after He ascended to the Father He would send the Holy Spirit who would dwell in us,[49] teach,[50] and guide us[51] into all truth. Now that He has been given to the Church, we live at a higher spiritual plane than those people of old.

Jesus explained with His coming to earth, a new day had dawned. The former law declared it a sin to commit adultery or murder, but a higher principle was now in effect: we are neither to lust nor hate.[52] In former times, the law laid down strict rules, and God led His people like young children who had not yet discovered His true nature. Now that we have the Light of the Gospel, we are to walk at a higher level of maturity than those who lived in earlier days.[53]

The way in which our walk is parallel to that of the people of Israel is this: we must pay attention. They had to watch: "Is the pillar moving or staying?" Our perception must be even more sharp. Instead of looking outwardly toward a physical guide, we focus instead on the Guide who dwells within.

Developing the patience to fully rely on the Lord to direct our path takes time. We're normally either so eager to "get on with it" or skeptical about whether those open doors are "of the Lord" that we're tempted to take our future into our own hands. Be careful!

Many of us know this verse by heart:

> *Trust in the LORD with all your heart, And lean not*
> *on your own understanding; In all your ways*
> *acknowledge Him, And He shall direct your paths.*
> (Proverbs 3:5-6)

If you can fully accept that, can you see how your stress level will move from fire-engine red to a calm and quieting pastel green? "Yes, but what if the Lord doesn't lead me?" Read the verse again. "He *shall* direct your paths!" When you draw near to God, He has promised to also draw near to you.[54]

Is God so feeble that He can't take hold of a little thing like you? Is He incapable of speaking to you or of causing your circumstances to so change that they force you to recognize "something out of the ordinary is happening"? The Holy Spirit will surely teach you if you seek His guidance. Lean in to hear the still, small voice of the Lord.[55] He isn't hiding, but He does want us to seek Him.

The heart of the matter is that we must not have our heads so buried in our own activities that we fail to be alert. It's not His job to tap us on the shoulder. It's up to *us* to watch, be vigilant, and follow as He directs our path. At times, it may not seem like a direct highway, but wherever He takes us will turn out to be the shortest possible route in preparation for all He has in store.

The Second Requisite: Obedience

In Exodus 16, three chapters after the first mandate to trust, we find the second requirement which is obedience. The story is that of God providing the strange new food, manna.

Just one month out of Egypt, and this crowd of people began to complain. They were running out of provisions. Now that seems like a pretty good reason for a complaint. Right?

As Moses brings the matter to the Lord, their complaining doesn't seem to upset God nearly as much as it does Moses! When it's time to give the people God's message, he does so all right, but adds his own two-cents worth as well. Moses tells the people:

"In the morning you shall see the glory of the LORD;
for He hears your complaints against the LORD.
But what are we,
that you complain against us?"
(Exodus 16:7, emphasis added)

This is the beginning of the miracle of manna appearing every morning for the next forty years. It continues along with quail to eat, at least periodically, until they cross the Jordan River and finally enter the Promised Land. God is now demonstrating to them that He is and will always be their Provider. *But*, there's a catch.

Then the LORD said to Moses, "Behold, I will rain bread
from heaven for you. And the people shall go out and gather
a certain quota every day, ***that I may test them,***
whether they will walk in My law or not."
(Exodus 16:4, emphasis added)

It's the easiest thing imaginable for God to supply whatever we need. Yet His manner of doing so is always tied in some way to developing our faith.

Everyday, they were to gather just enough for that day, and on the sixth day they were to gather enough to carry them over on the Sabbath. Not only did some disobey by trying to hoard, but on the seventh day, after God had told them there would be no manna and they should rest, some of the people went out looking for it anyway! Wasn't that blatant disobedience?

> *Now it happened that some of the people went out*
> *on the seventh day to gather, but they found none.*
> *And the LORD said to Moses, "How long do you refuse*
> *to keep My commandments and My laws?"*
>
> (Exodus 16:27-28)

Eventually, of course, they learned. We read no more of them violating this rule, even though they fed on the manna for the entire forty years. The story of this band of people repeatedly disobeying and then repenting, as God is trying to lead them to their appointed destiny, makes us wonder why and how God can be so patient. We read how those people acted, but we then see ourselves reflected in their behavior.

How long does it take us to learn? How often do we think doing what God says to do is not really a matter of obedience but just something for us to consider? We want God's blessing in our lives but so often refuse to obey.

Let's bring this home. Is there anything He's told you to do which you haven't done? Are there areas in your life where you're sincerely crying out to God for help—the stress meter is pegged at the top—and yet at the same time there are things you know God has said to do which you've considered optional or unimportant? What pops into your mind?

- "Repent and be baptized." Is it done?
- "Bring the tithes into the storehouse." Done?
- "If your brother has anything against you ... go be reconciled." Done?

Of course, these are just a sampling of things God may have set in front of you. His instructions are not there to restrict your life but to lead you to a place where you need not worry about anything. If *you* will (do whatever He says), then *He* will (do what He promised).[56] That includes (1) providing all you will ever need, and (2) leading your life to a fulfilling destiny. Taking action on whatever God speaks to you about brings freedom and blessing.

God cannot deliver you from unhealthy stress as long as you insist on maintaining control. He can and will increase what's in your hands when He can trust you to obey Him in managing what's already there.

It is required in stewards that one be found faithful.
(1 Corinthians 4:2)

Experience, it is said, is the best teacher, although I really don't want to learn everything the hard way! Yet finding the faith to trust, or the courage to act, often seems elusive. Let me tell you another story, this one about my breakdown regarding tithing. And don't panic! This is not a sidebar to get you to give. It isn't really about money at all. It will, I believe, illustrate how faith and courage work together.

As you now know from reading about my conversion experience, I was so afraid of not being able to live as a Christian that I immediately did whatever people told me I should do. That included tithing. When I began to bring my ten percent to the Lord—no big surprise—my financial life began to come together in ways I couldn't have imagined. Not in a day or a week, but within just a couple of months things started to change. It's not like the windows of heaven opened up, but it seemed I always had enough money for whatever I needed.

For many years, I grew and matured as a believer. Then there came a time in my life (and I hate to admit this) that I began to slip away from the disciplines I'd learned at the beginning. I still loved the Lord and considered myself a Christian, but eventually I stopped tithing. Very slowly, even though I was making a good salary and had the joy of receiving an inheritance, money seemed to slip through my hands. I found myself incapable of managing it well.

Finally there came a time when I repented of the detour I'd taken in my spiritual life. It may seem preposterous, but once again I had to go through the step-by-step process of deciding to trust God instead of my own thinking. And this time, in spite of all I'd seen earlier in my life, I struggled in trusting to tithe.

You see, I thought I couldn't afford it. Ha! Isn't that what everyone thinks? Each time I thought about obeying with that first ten percent of my income, it seemed to be at the worst possible moment. Either my cash flow was at low ebb, work was not available, or some big bill was looming in the near future. There was always something—the right time to begin simply never came.

I can't remember the date or situation, but one day I bit the bullet: "I'm going to do this!" That decision, just like the one at my conversion, was more a matter of calling on God in spite of myself than it was the spiritual act of a mature believer. No "gift of faith" in operation here. Just a bullheaded decision.

As a dormant seed is stimulated to grow when submerged in water, so the bullheaded act of doing what God asks us to do is all it takes. It's enough to trigger that mustard seed of faith into germination. Just by making a decision, our faith begins to grow.

Did the money start to pour in? No, of course not. I continued to struggle with my finances, but now I was making it through with the remaining 90 percent. In time, I came across people who could help me. Radio personalities inspired me to get out of debt; interviews on television suggested steps I could take; and books given as gifts began to help my thinking.

Little by little the finances in my life began to stabilize. I'm still not wealthy and have to manage my money, but I've never been in a situation where I didn't have enough. And that terrifying panic of approaching doom went away. Slowly but surely, the needle on my stress meter fell back toward normal. Pressures remain, but they're now a much healthier stress.

It's still up to me to manage whatever money I have. I still must be careful to not spend more than I earn. I must commit to never borrow money. I still must plan my giving so I don't become foolish in my good intentions. And so it goes. My ability to give to others, however, has increased, and all my needs have been met just as God promised.

I hope you can see how my story about tithing isn't really about money. It's about making the tough decision to act upon what God has said. First of all trusting Him to know what's best, and then obeying, without second-guessing on our part.

Concluding Thought ...

As with the children of Israel, it's not just a matter of "packing up and getting there." The journey for us, too, is that of moving from slavery to the Promised Land. And part of the purpose of the trip is so we will learn to trust and obey.

The Believer's Role

As Managers

For Discussion:

- Can you identify one area in your life where it seems you just can't achieve strength and solid footing? Anything outside of the area of finance?
- Why do you think Jesus and the entire Bible refer so much to financial management?
- How are you trusting God to lead you?
- In what ways have you put off obeying God or what the Scripture teaches?

What Action Steps Can You Take?

-
-
-
-

Chapter 9

Managing Yourself

"My thoughts are not your thoughts,
Nor are your ways My ways," says the LORD.
"For as the heavens are higher than the earth,
So are My ways higher than your ways,
And My thoughts than your thoughts."

(Isaiah 55:8, 9)

A new believer has much in common with those newly freed Israelis we read about in the last chapter. Like those people, each of us must leave the familiar and step out into new territory. And the new territory does not only apply to our environment, but to the change needed within us.

Captivity, oppression, and slavery are among the most debilitating conditions ever inflicted upon humankind. Although they'd been liberated, these people coming out of Egypt did not yet know how to think or act as free men and women. We need look no further than the aftermath of the civil war in our own country for a vivid example of the confused plight of a newly emancipated people. "Where do we go now? What shall we do? How will we provide for our children? Who will protect us?"

Of course, they too simply wanted to get to their new destination. The journey, on the other hand, would also include time to allow for a transformation in their thinking.

Turning away from old patterns of thought is one of the most difficult things to accomplish. Everyone who has ever tried to change a bad habit, lose weight, or made New Year's resolutions will surely agree to that.

The ability to manage anything begins with the ability to manage ourselves: our thoughts, emotions, relationships, vocation, and of course, our assets. Those who crossed the Red Sea had to learn a new way of thinking, and so do we. We all came from somewhere in the Dark into God's family. And the Scripture makes it clear: His thinking is not our thinking. No matter who we are and how clear and correct our thinking seems to us, we can't always trust it. We must learn to challenge it.

Consider how you became the person you now are. Even by the time you were a young child, you'd experienced both good and bad things. Your thinking, along with your emotions, was shaped by your culture, environment, parents, and teachers. That's true for all of us. Can you accept that much of the input you received was neither correct nor healthy? That's a fact.

Most loving and well-intended adults also transmit detrimental thought patterns, programmed emotional responses, and bad decision making. In addition to the many good things we were taught, those harmful patterns were also assimilated. Add to that the damaging patterns of our own making and ... there we are!

But listen, whoever gets the praise or the blame for impacting who we've become—our development need not stop where it is. We've heard for most of our lives that we can become whatever we choose, and that's true. It only takes deliberate awareness to modify the patterns we have succumbed to.

Have you suffered sadness, regret, hurts, and disillusionment? Those are things that *did* happen. But none of those things have the right or the power to alter who you are, unless you let them. Life's not over. We can change. It takes a bold look at ourselves, though, to examine how we came to be this way.

Manage Your Thinking

Every person believes his or her thinking to be good and correct. Don't you believe *your* thinking is correct? I feel confident mine is! So if you and I don't agree on something, whose idea is right? How can we tell? It's obvious we *both* can't be right. On the other hand, in all likelihood, neither of us is completely wrong.

Acquiring better thinking patterns requires our willingness to consider other contrasting viewpoints. If we aren't always right, it stands to reason the conclusions, opinions, and values we have accepted as true may also not be completely accurate. Some of those positions come from thinking patterns we've repeated, over and over again, without conscious thought. Therefore, they *sound* right to us—inside our brain.

Even negative thoughts about ourselves can sound "right" to us. Do you sometimes scold yourself for being stupid, careless, fat, lazy, accident prone, or something else? Do you remember someone else saying those things about you? We sometimes repeat what we heard as a child as if it were factual, without asking ourselves if we agree with it. Racial prejudice, political views, and numerous other values we embrace are often accepted without question.

Well, how do we correct our thinking? One way is to set aside time to do just one thing: *think*. Thoughts, of course, are going through our heads all day long. Those uninvited thoughts are sometimes helpful, often wasteful, and occasionally harmful. A good way to put our brain to productive use is to give it a deliberate, structured, and focused assignment. Review your values and prejudices. Define goals that will move your life forward. I'd like to share a couple of helpful exercises.

As a young man, I listened on the radio to the motivational speaker, Earl Nightingale. From the many inspirational things he taught, I learned and continue to practice the following two disciplines which have greatly impacted my life:

- The first requires sitting down to deliberate thinking. The technique is simply to commit 15 minutes a day to thinking deliberately about just one subject or idea. I do it first thing in morning over a cup of coffee, before my mind engages with work to be done, while the house is yet quiet, and before I pray.

  Take a sheet of paper, and write as the heading the topic you'll examine. List all the corresponding thoughts that come to you, both negative and positive. Consider if there are other ways to think about the subject. Turn the sentences around, expand on them, and ask yourself what you believe about the topic and why you do so. Then, as you read the Scripture, pray, listen to sermons and the like, you'll be amazed at the new thoughts that come to you. You'll find your thinking not only changed but also becoming stronger. You'll start to feel much better about the values you live by.

- The second calls for nailing those thoughts down to specific objectives. The technique is to ask what you want to accomplish about any project, or what habit or concern you'd like to change or develop. Be very specific about what you want to see and by when you want it done. Setting goals is very important.

Most of us have heard that a thousand times. Earl used an analogy that made the process clear and easy for me. It was the illustration of the captain of an ocean liner. A man with that responsibility would never leave a port without knowing his destination, route, and planned time of arrival. He has only *one* destination for each trip, one port-of-call, and he stays on course until he gets there.

How many times have you tried to go in several directions with lots of goals which ended up no more than something you'd *hoped* to accomplish? What is your next "port of call?" As you consider the next most important objective for you right now, picture it as a destination. That's where you're going. If there are stops along the way, that's fine—as long as they aren't detours.

A current example for me is finishing this book. Many other things call for my attention. Furthermore, no one is holding me accountable. There is no "boss" who will fire me if I don't work on my book today or finish it by such-and-such date. I am the only pilot of this ship. Turning a deaf ear to all the other things I want to do or that call for my attention must be done if I plan to arrive at my destination by my appointed time.

Actively managing your thinking process may be a new experience for you. It was for me, and it won't ever be completed. I continue to find new information, different points of view, and new topics to think through. It has become enjoyable, something I look forward to each morning. I even refer to it as "my coffee time with Earl."

There's one more piece to this that's critical. The final step in the project is to expose my thoughts and conclusions to others. I've learned it's very possible to believe that I've come up with a valuable and solid concept, only to have others I trust point out the holes in my theory.

My closest friend, Jerry King, does me such a valuable service by always being honest with me. He's never mean, but he also doesn't pull any punches. There are times when I'm inspired, explaining with enthusiasm why this or that is just the best plan ever, and his response goes, "Harold, that's the dumbest idea I've ever heard." Ha! I admit it's pretty disheartening. Yet, oh, so helpful. When that happens, it's back for another cup of coffee with Earl!

Verify the Accuracy of Your Thinking

The only way I know to *test* whether my thinking is solid and reliable is to come out of seclusion. Most of us would never think of ourselves as living in seclusion. After all, people are around us all the time. Television, movies, the internet and social networks put us more in touch with people than any other time in human history. Many if not most of those people, however, are more like acquaintances. We share small talk, jokes, occasionally ask a question, but we don't probe into testing solid thinking.

Who are the people in your life with whom you share your hopes, dreams, and troubles? Can you name at least one person who challenges your thinking?

The Bible teaches us not to forsake gathering together as believers.[57] The intent of that admonition isn't just for you to fellowship. It's for you to *connect* with other believers. Make friends with some of those people and find occasion to discuss the topics you're working on. Whenever you're in a group, encourage discussion. People *like* to think together. Even in a customary small group meeting, a sure way of killing inspiration is for one person to do all the talking. A far better approach is to present an idea and let people kick it around. Discuss other ways to think about or apply the lesson.

Let me add one more layer onto this. How diverse are the people you meet with? Most of the time, we choose to associate with those individuals from a similar socio-economic background, age group, political or religious belief. Conversations prevalent in that setting are often affirming rather than challenging. When we select additional groups of people to spend time with, those who are different from us—it's less comfortable—but our thinking matures even further.

What groups do you meet with outside of your core church groups? There are so many venues for us to connect with others that can be great fun: book clubs, sports activities, workout buddies at a gym, college extension classes, political movements, and so on. Most of them offer free membership. Joining one or more of these groups can be great fun. It will make you more interesting and expand your sphere of influence.

Of course, the Bible's admonition not to walk "in the counsel of the ungodly"[58] must be kept in mind. But there are many unbelievers who don't fit into that "ungodly" category. Some of the most influential and helpful people I've known weren't believers. That's sad, but there's no reason to avoid them. And to sequester oneself in the comfort of just church folks is to lose out on a great benefit.

Manage Your Emotions

Managing the way we feel may be an even more difficult area over which to gain control. It's far easier to try to change the way we think about something than it is to change the way we feel about it. Why? Because our emotional response was learned so early on in life, it seems to us involuntary. Like breathing, it just happens on its own.

We hear people say, "I couldn't help it. I just felt ...." What's the meaning behind the statement? We often hear that kind of talk when someone uses it as an alibi for something said or done which was unwise. Now they want something to blame (other than themselves) for their behavior.

First, can we agree that how we feel and how we behave are two separate issues? When two children are playing alone together and the older takes a toy from the younger, what's the response of the younger? Anger! Immediately! He may try to hit his sibling or throw a toy at him.

If mom or dad is in the room, won't he modify his behavior? Oh yes. Watch his face and you'll see the anger still rises immediately. This time, though, he checks himself. Without the attempted swat or tossing of the toy, he looks at his parent with a wounded expression and howls, "He took my toy!"

Don't we behave the same way even after becoming adults? When somebody has "done me wrong," I may be relating the atrocity to my close buddy about that "stupid, unthoughtful, arrogant..." But what's my reaction when that "somebody" walks into the room? (You get the picture.) I put a lid on my tirade, of course. A lifted eyebrow aimed at my friend may indicate I'll tell more later, but for now the story is over.

We monitor our behavior as adults just as children do. We may be red in the face about one infringement or another and then speak as calmly as a counselor to the offending person when we see them. Feeling the way we do is different than how we choose to behave.

The issue at hand is how to *change* how we feel. The idea that feelings cannot be controlled, that we're helpless victims of that tyrant, is simply not true. We may not yet have learned how, but the tools to do so are at hand.

Nonetheless, what's definitely true about our feelings is that they are automatic and immediate—BOOM! We can't help the fact those feelings slam right into us, welcome or not.

Someone once helped me understand what happens with our emotions and how to make adjustments. Let's look at the table below:

Automatic Thought	Controlled Thought
Automatic Emotion	Controlled Emotion
Automatic Behavior	Controlled Behavior

Our automatic thoughts create automatic emotions, which in turn result in automatic behavior. In order to turn those into controlled thoughts, emotions, and behaviors, the automatic cycle must be interrupted.

In any situation, when an incident that's similar to what we may have seen before happens, our response is automatic. All previous experiences are recorded in our minds along with an interpretation of what we believe to be their meaning. The small child who had the toy taken from him reacted immediately because he knew what that meant: his rights had been violated. Take a toy from a baby, however, and there's no emotional response at all. He hasn't yet learned about rights.

Once a young child learns what "taking" means, the action causes an automatic feeling of offense. As his older sibling may have demonstrated how to behave when violated, he now also knows how to behave. From that point on, it's all automatic.

As we grew up, we've learned from those around us how we should feel and behave. Unless a situation is brand new to us, the thoughts, feelings, and behaviors come instinctively. We're programed to behave in ways manifested by our parents, teachers, and older siblings. Without speaking a word, they taught us. And unless you've taken steps to think through how you want to live differently, you're most likely a reflection of those whose lifestyle you observed.

You can't prevent your mind from automatically interpreting what happens, and the thought-emotion reaction is almost simultaneous. The feelings that rise you truly cannot help.

How do you alter the course of action? The key is to interrupt the process at the middle point—automatic emotion. Here's how. Train yourself to recognize or "catch" the automatic emotion as soon as possible. Sooner or later you'll discover that *acknowledging* what you feel interrupts the circuitry.

As an exercise, think of something that sets you off. "When this or that happens I get so ... (angry, frustrated, disappointed, etc.)." Now tell yourself the next time it happens you'll recognize and say it, either out loud or under your breath, "That makes me angry!"

Those words will engage your controlled thinking from the right-hand column of the table. Because you have to think them, the words you speak cause your brain to be in the "now" instead of in the past. That, in turn, opens the door to making a decision, a choice about how you'll behave and what action you'll take.

Making a *conscious* decision will also affect how you feel. After some time, you'll discover that you don't react the same way you used to. Instead of being the victim of an automatic feeling, you now have control. Even though the triggering situation will remain the same, your response will have changed. In fact, *you* will have changed. "I couldn't help it" will no longer stand as an acceptable excuse, as you *can* take charge of how you feel.

Manage Your Commitments

Everything we've become is directly related to decisions we've made in the past. Most of the things we decide throughout the day, though, are really no longer decisions. They're habits—how we take care of personal hygiene, our eating, social skills, and so on are all done without requiring new thought or commitment.

Other major decisions pertaining to your vocation, marriage, children, and ministry require a deliberate and continued commitment. Some of those decisions may have been made long ago, but they're things you're still committed to. To a large degree, they delineate the path you now walk.

What role does God play in those things? In some cases, He wasn't yet in our lives when we made this or that decision. A few things just came in without invitation. Still others became part of our lives because of some unfortunate or stupid choices we had made. Regardless of how things came to be, we're responsible to deal with them now. A good steward doesn't resign or abrogate responsibility. Instead, he determines to make increasingly better decisions and faithfully manage to his best ability.

As a manager, you must make decisions. God wants you to. He planned it that way. And once the decision has been made, the commitment to maintain that obligation continues. Did you marry, conceive a child, buy a field, or enter into partnership with others? Each of those decisions call upon your time, effort, money, and thought—for either as long as the relationship exists or until the Master returns.

What, my friend, is in your hand to manage? What commitments have you made? How are you doing in managing yourself so your efforts will be productive and rewarding?

God has given us amazing abilities to think, reason, plan, and create—just like Him! It's *natural* for us to always be searching for new and better ways to do things. He wants us to be bold in exercising those abilities but only after learning through obedience to trust that His ways will always be better than our ways. The principles that govern the spiritual universe are as foundational and reliable as the ones that govern our physical world. Learning to rely on those principles only comes about through practice and experience.

Concluding Thought ...

You'll find it worthwhile to make a list of those long-term commitments you've made. Having your own "coffee with Earl" will help you direct your thoughts. Remember what Jesus said,

> *"For which of you, intending to build a tower,*
> *does not sit down first and count the cost,*
> *whether he has enough to finish it—lest,*
> *after he has laid the foundation, and is not able to finish,*
> *all who see it begin to mock him."*
>
> (Luke 14:28-29)

The Believer's Role

Managing Yourself

For Discussion:

- Consider your journey from the day you accepted Christ as Savior until now. Have you had to change your thinking from that of a slave to a free man or woman?

- What are some of the beliefs you were taught from childhood that you no longer believe? Are there still lingering doubts that sometimes make you feel trapped?

- Have you ever done an exercise like the "coffee with Earl?" If so, share your experience and discuss the process.

- Can you describe some area in which you feel stuck in the automatic thought/feeling/behavior cycle? How do you think you could catch yourself at the automatic feeling stage?

What Action Steps Can You Take?

Chapter 10

Managing What Is in Your Hands

Work willingly at whatever you do, as though you were working for the Lord rather than for people.

(Colossians 3:23, NLT)

What do you have to manage, right now? Take an inventory. I think you'll find it boils down to relationships, activities, and assets.

Create and Develop Relationships

Everything you'll ever accomplish will be done through people. You can't build a business, create a family, sell a product, or earn a living without the help and involvement of others.

There's only very little that's more important than the people in our lives. Nevertheless, not much of our energy is used to take care of existing and developing relationships.

Review a list of those you're involved with. Every relationship must be managed or it will stagnate, and don't forget that part of stagnation is putrefaction. Nothing stays fresh when it lies dormant. A neglected relationship will not completely spoil, but it will become far less vibrant than it used to be.

A number of years ago, I learned about the We Bridge. In any relationship—family, siblings, friends—a We Bridge is created. Think of each person as owning a circle of space. When we form a relationship with someone else, the two circles are brought together. The two circles of space not only connect to one another but now also overlap.

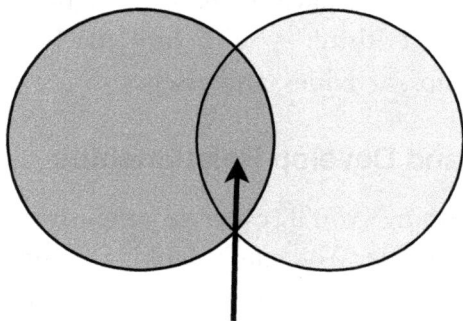

The overlapping area has created a We Bridge. We have, by consent, entered each other's space. The sharing of that space with someone else can be delightful or terrible. Understanding its existence supplies us with the ability to manage our shared space.

And to keep a relationship from going sour, it's imperative we remain aware of and respect that Bridge.

Let's use marriage as an example. No closer human relationship exists than that of a husband and wife. The Bible says, *"they shall become one flesh."*[59] Closer than brother and sister, closer than parent and child, the husband and wife were designed to become one. Yet they remain different individuals. There's the rub. How can two people, each with their own mind, will, hopes, and dreams function as a single unit?

Some of our decisions will either benefit or hurt our spouse. Other decisions won't affect our spouse at all. If I choose to play golf instead of tennis, my wife doesn't care. She's unaffected. If she has pasta instead of a salad for lunch, I don't care. I'm unaffected. On the other hand, if I turn on the television in the same room where she is trying to read, she *is* affected. If she decides to vacuum while I'm trying to take a nap, *I'm* affected. We're breaching each other's space in the latter scenarios. We're violating the We Bridge.

The same applies not only with other individuals but also in our spiritual life. God has "married" us for eternity, yet He has also given us the ability to make individual decisions. Some of our decisions will not impact the holiness of that relationship one way or the other. Those that affect our sacred union, however, will bring either honor or disgrace to both our identity and His.

Understanding the We Bridge helps us understand what may be "wrong" in our relationship with children, parents, siblings, and others. When relationships either cool or become overheated, almost always the We Bridge has been violated. One or both of us may not be respecting the shared space created by our bond.

If you need to repair a relationship, remember the only person you can manage is you. If you recognize you've been the violator, admit it, and ask for forgiveness. When you do, presto, you've opened the way to restoration. Be careful with discussing the We Bridge. Avoid talking about the other person's violation of your space. Make sure you aren't trying to manage the other person. Instead, let him or her know of your intent to restore the relationship. That's enough to make a point. Doing more may lead to blaming. And that's no way to build a bridge.

Keep Your Activities Balanced

You might think of activities as simply the things you do. How are you using the time that's been given you? Is anything being built or created? Or are you just keeping time, marching in place, experiencing little change in life?

When we spend our time, we are choosing how to spend our lives. Some activities are not optional. Time must be given to sleeping, eating, and caring for the necessities of life. Beyond that, the time we spend on work, play, self-development, entertainment, and the like are choices we make. These choices, of course, reflect what's most important to us—our values.

What's happening with your vocation? Students, homemakers, brain surgeons, or mechanics are all made in the image of God. They are creators.

How creative are you? If you don't see your career path improving, what's the problem? If you don't like the job you're currently in, how long will you stay in that position? Once you know you aren't fitted to a certain job, it's time to consider how to get from where you are to a better place. Often, getting into something new is easier than making the decision to do it.

It may be that you're working at one job and desire to be in another that requires a skill set you've not yet achieved. Why not start developing those skills in your spare time? It's a matter of continuing education. Whether applied to formal schooling or your career path, in order to become more effective you'll have to learn new skills.

For several years, I pastored a church in Springfield, Illinois. I was young and therefore would cut myself some slack, but I have to admit that I wasn't a very good pastor. It's not that I didn't love people. I just didn't know how to serve them better. My skills hadn't yet developed. I learned so much more, many years later, while working alongside genuinely skilled pastors.

I could use that same illustration in every job I ever held. Upon learning about planned giving (using charitable remainder trusts and the like to avoid taxation and increase income) I was mentored by a very successful man. We worked together at a prestigious hospital in La Jolla, California. I was so fortunate having him at my side.

My education, however, didn't stop there. A couple of years later, a much larger foundation hired me to create a planned giving department from scratch. Working with a mentor was one thing, this was another. Fortunately, all my life I've tried to continue learning. Having studied a number of books and teachings written by the famous Peter Drucker, the management guru, helped me beyond measure.

As I sat in my new office thinking about where to start, I remembered something he'd written: if you want to be a leader in any arena, research until you find five people who are at the head of the pack in your industry. Meet with each of them, if possible, but find out what they're doing that has so distinguished them.

Then, one-by-one, replicate what each of those five is doing. Of course, you won't be able to perform as well as they do, at least not right away. But two things will happen if you carry this out. First, you'll be employing five of the best tested strategies in your line of work that will soon put you at the top. The second benefit is that once you've accomplished those things, there won't be anyone else to follow! From that point on, you'll have to develop from there in your own unique way. Your creative abilities will now come alive as you're forced to become innovative.

In my new planned giving post, I actually followed that course. I found five men with the most outstanding programs, met with them, and to the best of my ability replicated what they were doing. (These were all men outside of my city and, therefore, non-competitors.) The program we initiated became among the fastest planned giving startups in the world of healthcare fundraising.

My learning experience far exceeded the price of a book. But you get the point. Don't stop learning. Never be satisfied with your current role in life, in business, in relationships, or anything else. God created you to be an ever-growing entrepreneur of life.

What is it you want to be? Who are the role models who exemplify what you envision? Meet with them if you can, find out why they're effective, and duplicate what they do. As you learn the skills of those five different leaders you'll become something different than you've ever been.

Take Care of Your Assets

The principles we just talked about work the same in handling money and other assets. In chapter eight, you read the story of a woman who was offended with my sermon, when I made the comment that if there is an area in your life where you're relentlessly weak, it means that you haven't yet learned the lessons necessary to become strong in that area. In her case, that had to do with finances.

In counseling with people about financial concerns, most of the time I've found that people really didn't need additional advice. What they needed was to learn to separate the stress from the issue, so they could look squarely at their situation. They already knew how to decide. The problem was that they'd continued in denial, hoping the world would change, that God would provide a miracle, or in some other way they would be delivered from their dilemma. Isn't that almost like playing the lottery? Let me encourage you not to sit on your hands waiting for a piece of good fortune.

If you've made careless decisions and are now in a situation where you have more debt than you can handle, more home than you can afford, cars that are more egocentric than practical, you probably already know what to do. It may be time for a "come to Jesus talk."

I once worked for a woman who loved to use that phrase. Everybody knew what she meant, and she wasn't talking in religious terms. Repentance at any level involves the same process: we must confess that we've been wrong, be truly sorry for what we've done and the mess we've made of things, and then firmly decide to turn around. Almost all of us know the right thing to do. We just keep putting off the decision to get started.

Control Your Giving

Managing your giving is a subset of managing assets. But it's distinct enough to merit its own discussion. Here, I'm not referring to the tithe. The Bible says the first ten percent *belongs* to God. If you don't own it, you can't give it. Giving something that doesn't belong to you is a form of stealing.

Giving includes everything you give beyond your tithe, not only to the church but also to the additional charitable entities you support. Learning to give wisely requires as much skill as managing money in any other capacity. It's as important for you to learn to give with wisdom as it is to have an open heart. Too often I've seen believers classify giving and money management differently. Your compassion and love for God's work can mislead you into thinking that your gifts are to be generated by your emotions, not your mind.

Some people begin to give at an accelerated rate in the hopes that God will see their heart and bail them out of trouble. That's not the thinking of a good and skillful manager. It's related to denial.

Let me give you one illustration. I once met with a 74-year-old woman to discuss her giving. She'd seen an illustration I'd presented during a seminar on how retirement money could be used together with a charitable gift. At her age, the strategy could triple the income she was getting. This kind of charitable gift is irrevocable, would provide her with tax deductions, and the church would receive what was left in the account at the time of her death.

I wanted to make sure this gifting strategy was beneficial to her, and not just to the church. So I asked what other resources she had to live on. She began by telling me that she was giving away 60 percent of her income each month. "That's wonderful!" I said. "How much monthly income do you have?" And here's where the shock began.

Not only did she have quite a limited income, but her retirement account (the one she was considering giving into a charitable gift annuity) was also not large. When I learned there were very few additional assets outside of that, I explained the strategy she had in mind would be unwise for her. "Nonetheless," I said, "Tell me about your giving. You're being very generous."

She went on to explain that although her income was not large, she felt so much more fortunate than many others in the world. In addition to paying her tithe to the church, she was giving to various television ministries. She felt so moved and wanted to help the missionaries, orphan ministries, and so on. She then reminded me, "You can't out-give God!"

There are many such mottos, and even Bible verses, that can be terribly misapplied. When I asked how she was paying her bills, she explained that when utility bills or insurance payments were due, she would use her credit cards. They were getting close the limit now, but God would provide.

For a while, I just sat there feeling sad and asking God for wisdom of what to say. Before me sat a godly and very sincere believer who was hurting herself in the cause of the Lord. As gently as I could, I looked into her eyes and told her that I needed to say some things to her that would be difficult for her to hear. It might even sound strange to her. So I encouraged her to talk to her pastor about it so he could advise her as well.

We then spent our time together talking about being a wise steward. God had *already* provided for her. Even after paying her tithe, He'd given her all the money she needed to live and take care of herself. Now, however, she was driving herself into debt because of her good heart. "It's not my job to tell anyone else what they *should do*," I told her. And then I talked to her about the principles that you've read in this book.

As sad as that story is, there's a happy ending. A little over a year later, that same church invited me back to minister with them for a few days again. After speaking on a Wednesday night, guess who came up to the front to say hello. It was my 74-year-old friend.

"Harold," she said. "I just wanted to come up and thank you. You may not even remember our talk, but I was the woman who ...." In fact, I didn't recognized her right away, but I did remember the story. She went on to explain that she'd thought about the matter and prayed carefully about it. She continued to tithe but had cut back on her giving. "But not altogether," she whispered with a smile.

She then told me that she was now living within her means, no more use of credit cards, and would be out of debt before the year was over. I don't how that makes you feel, but I've just got to say "Hallelujah!"

One of these days, it might take a year or two, that woman will have the financial ability to give in a way she's not known before. It will come from her abundance, not just from compassion, guilt, or trying to press God to give out even more.

It's helpful to remember the basics when your emotions are stirred. Who owns it all? God does. So when you give, remember that what He's put into your hands is for you to manage, not distribute as if it were your own. If you carefully weigh all the factors of a gift in light of what God is doing in your life, and you believe He would be pleased with your response, then by all means give. Just be a good manager of what you now have.

Stay alert to popular preachers who may not "rightly divide the Word of God." It's not necessary to criticize them, but be careful that the decisions you make are balanced on the entire Bible, not just on a few verses. I've heard some, several of whom I respect in other areas, say some pretty outrageous things. Be careful about giving your last dollar, the application of "seed money" gifts, and other appeals that aim at your emotions. Instead of giving or committing right away, make a note to give it serious thought. Pray. And talk to your pastor about it. Certainly, you want to stay open to the leading of the Holy Spirit and always be obedient to God. Yet if a gift you are considering seems to be out of line for your lifestyle, get the confidential advice of elders who love both you and the Lord.

Concluding Thought ...

God has called you to be a manager. The better you do in managing what's now in your hands, not only will the Lord give you more to manage, but the stress meter will remain in its healthy zone. He's not just trying to see something develop in your life temporarily. He wants you to work effectively with Him throughout all of eternity.

Start now. There's work to do, but whether it's managing money, assets, relationships, your career, or any other thing, He's promised to walk through it with you.

The Believer's Role

Managing What's in Your Hands

For Discussion:

- With whom do you share a We Bridge?
- Can you think of some times when you've violated that bridge with someone? Can you share what you did?
- What are the most difficult activities for you to keep in balance? What steps could you take to correct the imbalance.
- Are there skills you could develop or classes you could take that would advance you to a higher level? In what areas?
- Discuss giving beyond the tithe. Have you ever given too much? Do you think it's possible to give too much? How could a person weigh that issue to make sure the decision is one of a good manager?

What Action Steps Can You Take?

Part 3
The Believer's Role

Let's Summarize:

The two roles God has given to every believer are to represent Him as His ambassador and to manage whatever He allows to be put into our hands. These roles are more easily understood when we look at how they function in our everyday world. Here's what they look like in summary.

Ambassadors

When Jesus announced the Great Commission to go into all the world to spread the Gospel, He ordained us as His Ambassadors. The only representatives the unbelieving world will know of our God are what we carry forward. Yet God didn't intend for that to be an ominous assignment. It should be as natural for us as being a good citizen and representative of our country.

A good citizen will study his country's history, laws, and the principles upon which it was founded. And so when asked about how his country is governed and why, his answers will be accurate only to the degree that he's matured in knowledge.

Regardless of how deep or shallow the ability he has to represent his nation, he can always testify as to what it's like to be a citizen of his homeland. After all, he's lived there. His experiences will be somewhat different than that of another citizen, but he knows what he's seen, heard, and experienced. That personal testimony is enough to give witness to what's it's like to be a member of his nation.

Now that you and I are citizens of God's Kingdom, we are qualified right now to testify of our own experience with God. As we learn and become better trained (discipled), we can help those who are young or uneducated to develop. Finally, we may stand as an exemplary representative of our God—an ambassador.

What a privilege, and what a position we can aspire to attain!

Managers

The principle taught in the Scripture is clear and simple: if you manage whatever you now have, you'll be given more. It's not at all mystical. It isn't even necessary to be spiritually minded to understand. That principle works in our everyday world just as it does in God's kingdom.

Any owner must have confidence that his managers will be faithful. If you would be a manager, it is mandatory that you be faithful in allowing the owner to direct your work and your future, and also that you'll do as you're told; that is, obey. How we are to conduct ourselves as managers boils down to simple common sense.

A manager must first develop the ability to manage himself. Learning to move beyond the habits and thought patterns he was taught as a child is the first step. Determined to manage his own thinking, the manager learns to control not only his behavior but the emotions that trigger the behavior.

Now, fully in charge of his own thinking, he can bring all his abilities to bear on every asset put under his oversight. He will develop his relationships with others, balance the way he uses his time, and creatively handle money and assets to advance the owner's domain.

Afterword

This book is the first volume of a two-part series. Initially, I began writing the book, *Financially Prosperous Believers*. Meeting so many who seemed stopped in their tracks by the looming stress bully, I decided to write this book first.

There are many lessons we can all learn to become even *better* stewards of what God gives us. Those practical steps are covered in the next volume. If you'd like to be notified when book two is available, register at www.HaroldMetzel.com.

Stress can be brutal. If left unchecked, it can block our faith and effectiveness. You can stop this progression by not allowing it to go so far that you feel like a victim. Stand up to it and like most bullies stress will back away.

In my life, I've stood up to it many times. It was hard to maintain a positive attitude when I didn't have enough money to meet my obligations, other times when people threatened me with a lawsuit, and still other times when I'd "invested" in a good deal and watched it go deeper and deeper into the tank. It was hard to keep my head up at times like these. I felt like a fool, a failure. And I was both ashamed and angry at myself for making such dumb decisions.

Here's what I learned, though, about separating the stress from the problem. The bully did back off. *But it didn't stay away.* A financial statement or notice might come in, and uninvited thoughts would come back into my mind. I'd start to feel sick all over again. "What am I going to do?"

The stress bully will come back as often as you allow it to. You must stand up to it again and again. As you do, you'll develop the ability to dismiss it more quickly and with greater ease.

Let me tell you one more rather strange but personal story. Shortly after my conversion, I had my first encounter with the devil. You may choose to believe this or not. There may not be a lot of theological argument to substantiate it. Nonetheless, I'm taking my own advice and simply acting as a witness.

When I became a Christian, I was advised to read the Bible and get on my knees and pray (out loud) every day. So before going to bed each night, I'd get on my knees at the bedside and pray. I hadn't developed a real prayer life yet. This was a five-to-ten minute "now I lay me down to sleep" type of prayer. After a week or so, while kneeling at the bed with my eyes closed, it seemed as if I could see the devil standing behind me. He didn't do anything except lean against the door jam and watch me.

Let me tell you, that was creepy. On several occasions, I jumped right into bed, deciding to skip the prayer because it felt very threatening to me. Now you may laugh, but when I did that, it seemed to me that the devil looked at me and smirked.

Here's how my deliverance took place. I told my pastor about the experience. He didn't tell me I was silly or try to talk me out of what I'd imagined. He simply told me that when Satan was cast out of heaven, he took a third of the angels with him. That means two of God's angels remained against each bad one that had left. A bad angel or demon had no power over me because I belong to God, and His angels are stronger and more numerous.

The next night, although afraid to even go to bed, I undressed, turned out the light, and got on my knees. Sure enough, there he was. So I echoed to God what the pastor had said. Then I prayed, "Whether it's real or not, would you please send your angels to make him leave?" Then, maybe all in my head, I saw two angels enter my room, take that devil under each arm, and carry him off. And that vision, real or not, never bothered me again.

While I have no intent to introduce a theological issue about angels or demons, I do know that the devil tempted and directly confronted Jesus. He tempted Him with malice but had no power or authority over Him. That's a true experience, but my understanding of angels and demons is probably no greater than yours.

The lesson I learned, however, and one that I hope will encourage you, is that stress can be treated in much the same way. Don't ignore it. Rather, realize that it has no *real* power. It's like the boogeyman under the bed—scary, but having no genuine power.

When we understand God's plan for the world and for each of us who now belong to Him, we can face whatever life throws at us. By fully grasping God's intent for us not to struggle in desperation but to represent Him and manage what He gives us, our personal stress meter will remain in healthy balance.

> *Now may the God of hope fill you with all joy and peace*
> *in believing, that you may abound in hope*
> *by the power of the Holy Spirit.*
>
> (Romans 15:13)

Acknowledgements

Everything we do is accomplished through people; even writing a book. As I've been helped by loved ones and friends, I want to express my deep gratitude to the following:

All of the pastors who invited me to speak to your congregation, thank you. I realize that an invitation to do so is a demonstration of trust. It was out of my experiences with you and your people that I felt motivated to write this in the first place. I hope that the book will serve your congregation well.

My wife, Joan, who I've learned is among the best of editors. I'm grateful not only for your technical skills but also for your insight and instinctive awareness to know when something wasn't expressed quite right. Your patience has been a great asset to me.

My friends, Janice Dawson, Jerry and Jennie King, for your willingness to volunteer those hours to edit and then proofread the text once again. Your input made the book more credible.

Those teachers of writing I've learned so much from. How grateful I am for those who have written books, conducted seminars, and mentored me along the way. Most of all, to Gary Provost who passed away much too soon.

My coach, Kathy Carlton-Willis, who has helped me through the maze of knowing what to do next.

My professional editor, Nymfa Aranas, who has been both thorough and encouraging every step of the way. I've felt not only the strength of your skills but your passion for the Church as we've worked together.

Share With Your Small Group

DVD Study Resource Guide

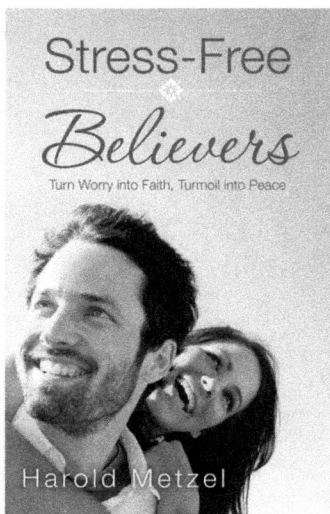

Stress-Free
Believers
Turn Worry into Faith, Turmoil into Peace

Harold Metzel

On this DVD, the author puts forth a mindset for studying each chapter of the book. Every one of the 5-10 minute topics offers a case study to stimulate further discussion.

This valuable resource will make the study sessions more practical, whether used in small group study, men's or women's groups, youth groups, or other church discussion groups.

This DVD, audio book, and other resources can be ordered at:

StressFreeBelievers.com

Share With Friends

If you like this book, share it with others who may be going through significant stress. Many people buy this book not for themselves but for sisters and brothers, parents and children, and friends who are going through difficult times.

After speaking on the topic of "Dethroning the Stress Bully," I received an email message from one of the men who had attended the service. He wrote:

> Harold, thank you for your encouraging message. One of my volunteers who received the message on CD because she served in the nursery the night you preached, said that your teaching helped her work with her high school age daughter's school stress cycle. They have listened to your teaching over and over and pray every morning before the daughter goes to school.

Isn't that great! I've often been the recipient of books and CDs that people gave to me. Many of those I probably would never have found on my own.

If you know of people who are going through trying times—the sick, shut-ins, the elderly—or others going situations that create great stress or fear, consider getting copies of this book, or even this audio book, as gifts. And if you do decide to buy several, remember that quantity discounts are available on the website.

Notes

1 Romans 8:31

2 Matthew 13:22

3 http://www.stlyrics.com/lyrics/lifeasahouse/bothsidesnow.htm

4 Rabbi Daniel Lapin. *Thought Tools*, 2008, (Lifecodex Publishing, Mercer Island, WA 2008), 160

5 New Spirit Filled Life Bible, Thomas Nelson Bibles, Nashville, TN, 2002), 1756

6 http://www.bartleby.com/119/1.html

7 I John 1:8

8 http://thinkexist.com/quotation/
faith_is_believing_in_things_when_common_sense/180914.html

9 Hebrews 11:6

10 Matthew 21:22

11 Ephesians 6:12

12 Matthew 14:28

13 Matthew 6:10

14 Mark 9:24

15 Proverbs 30:32

16 Genesis 17:17

17 Earl Nightingale. *Lead The Field*, (Nightingale Conant Corporation, Niles, Illinois,) Audio Recording.

18 Ibid

19 James 5:14-15

Notes

20 http://www.noogenesis.com/pineapple/blind_men_elephant.html (April 30, 2011)

21 Genesis 1:1

22 Genesis 2:17

23 Ephesians 1:4

24 Luke 18:22

25 Matthew 6:24

26 New Spirit Filled Life Bible, (Thomas Nelson Bibles, Nashville, TN, 2002) 1,652

27 John 16:5-15

28 John 13:29

29 Matthew 6:9-13

30 Mark 1:15

31 Luke 17:21

32 Joshua 1:9

33 Philippians 4:19

34 Acts 1:9-11

35 Acts 2:39

36 John 17:14-19

37 Matthew 5:16

38 John 16:8

39 Matthew 6:1-7

40 John Amstutz, Disciples of All Nations, (Foursquare Media, Los Angeles, CA, 2009) p.46

Notes

41 Matthew 18:20

42 Ephesians 4:12

43 Hebrews 10:24-25

44 Kenneth C. Ulmer. *Making Your Money Count*, (Regal Books, Ventura, CA 2007) p. 41

45 Matthew 25:21

46 Matthew 5:45

47 Laaren Brown, Lenny Hort, and Eric Thomas. *Children's Illustrated Jewish Bible* (DK Publishing, Inc., New York, NY 1997)

48 David S. Dockery, Ed. *Dolman Bible Handbook*, (Holman Bible Publishers, Nashville, TN, 1992)

49 John 16:13

50 John 14:26

51 John 16:13

52 Matthew 5:17-22

53 Romans 7:6-25

54 James 4:8

55 I Kings 19:12

56 2 Chronicles 7:14

57 Hebrews 10:25

58 Psalm 1:1

59 Genesis 2:24

www.ingramcontent.com/pod-product-compliance
Lightning Source LLC
Chambersburg PA
CBHW070957040426
42443CB00007B/542